Toward
a Theory
of Instruction

Toward
a Theory
of Instruction

By JEROME S. BRUNER

THE BELKNAP PRESS OF
1966   HARVARD UNIVERSITY PRESS
CAMBRIDGE · MASSACHUSETTS

Distributed in Great Britain by
Oxford University Press, London

The research for this book was supported in part by grants
from the U.S. Public Health Service (#5T1–GM–1011 and
#MH05120). It was further supported through the Coopera-
tive Research Program of the U.S. Office of Education under
contract #OE4–10–136.

Library of Congress Catalog Card Number 66–13179

Printed in the United States of America

In Memory of
Francis Friedman

whose vision
helped all of us to see

Preface

This book came into being over a period of five years. Each of the essays has gone through its own metamorphosis. The first draft of one essay would lead to a change in the second draft of another, and, in the end, they might get fused. All but the last essay have been through at least three such reciprocal versions, some through as many as six. So while the essays were each written "separately" they have lived long together in the community of my thoughts. The unity they possess comes from· half a decade of coping with the problems they undertake.

They are not technical papers, though the echo of technical concerns sounds through them all. Nor are they casual papers, for they were produced under the press of practical need. During the years of their writing, I was engaged not only in research on development, but also in teaching young children in classrooms, in constructing curricula even to the editing of films, in teaching teachers—in short, in the practical tasks of public education. I have also served on the Panel on Educational Research and Development at the White House, goaded into hypotheses by our demanding chairman, Jerrold Zacharias. The essays are, in effect, the efforts of a student of the cognitive processes trying to come to grips with the problems of education.

Parts of these essays and of others that were fused in making them have been given as lectures: as Sigma Xi Lecture at Yale in 1965; as presidential addresses to the Society for the Psy-

chological Study of Social Issues in 1964 and the American
Psychological Association in 1965; as an address at the Educational Testing Service in Princeton in 1964; as the Ruth
Tolman Memorial Lecture at Los Angeles in 1965; as Jen-
nings Scholar Lecture in Cleveland in 1964; as Eaton Lecture
at Syracuse University in 1963; as a speech at the Colloquium
of the Center for Cognitive Studies in 1964; and as an address
at the conference of the National Council of Teachers of
English in 1963.

Some of the themes that find expression in the various essays
first came into my thoughts as a result of the discussions that
took place at a lively conference sponsored by the President's
Science Advisory Committee, Panel on Educational Research
and Development, on the theme of learning and development.
The conference was held at Harvard for a fortnight during the
summer of 1963. It was underwritten by grants from the National Science Foundation and the U.S. Office of Education,
and its proceedings are to be published early in 1966 by the
latter organization under my editorship with the title *Learning
About Learning*.

None of the essays has been published in its present form.
In earlier versions, "Coping and Defending" appeared in
French under the title "Affrontement et défense" in the *Journal
de psychologie normale et pathologique,* Winter 1961; "Education as Social Invention" appeared in *The Journal of Social
Issues,* vol. 20, no. 3; "Notes on a Theory of Instruction" appeared in the Sixty-third Yearbook of the National Society
for the Study of Education, Part I, *Theories of Learning and
Instruction, 1964* (Chicago, 1964); "Man: A Course of Study"
appeared in the *ESI Quarterly Report,* Spring-Summer 1965.
I am grateful to these publications for permission to use these
papers.

I gladly take this opportunity to express my indebtedness
to several people. My colleague Professor George A. Miller

professes no special interest in matters pedagogical. Yet I find his thinking very germane and constantly arresting. My colleagues Professor Elting Morison, Professor Franklin Patterson, and Professor Morton G. White have taught me much about problems of education. Several colleagues with whom I have worked closely these last few years have been of great help, particularly Dr. David McNeill, Dr. Mary Henle, Dr. Margaret Donaldson, Mr. Norman Ross, and Mrs. Blythe Clinchy.

There are people with whom one becomes invisibly linked in a kind of internal monologue—one's own Old Guard. I have already mentioned Jerrold Zacharias. I should add David Hawkins, Philip Morrison, Sister Jacqueline Brennan, David Page, Frank Brown, and Robert Davis.

I have dedicated this book to Professor Francis Friedman, late Professor of Physics at the Massachusetts Institute of Technology. I realize now, in retrospect, that it was the patient wisdom of his questions that made me aware of what a theory of instruction might entail. His untimely death has left us blinder than we might have been.

Let me express my thanks to those who made work and life possible during the period over which the task of writing was extended. The curriculum research described in these pages was supported by the Ford Foundation and the National Science Foundation in grants to Educational Services, Inc. Grants from the National Institute of Mental Health, the Office of Education, and the Carnegie Corporation to the Center for Cognitive Studies at Harvard supported much of my own work. I am particularly indebted to Harvard for a year's leave to work on problems of pedagogy. I had the pleasure, during a month in the spring of 1965, of being Bacon Professor at the University of Aix-en-Provence, where I was able to finish much of the rewriting of this book and discuss its contents with colleagues there.

The Center for Cognitive Studies at Harvard has been the most patient—permitting me to wander for a year in Cambridge without ever intruding on my time or energy. Professor George Miller took over my duties, and Mrs. Lou Bartlett and Mrs. Ellen Plakans kept the ship provisioned.

Mrs. Maud Wilcox, Executive Editor of the Harvard University Press, has been a constant source of wisdom and encouragement in the final stages of the writing. As always, it has been my wife whose partnership in dialogue helped the ideas take shape.

Jerome S. Bruner

Cambridge, Massachusetts
7 November 1965

Contents

Toward
a Theory
of Instruction

Chapter I

Patterns
of Growth

INSTRUCTION IS, after all, an effort to assist or to shape growth. In devising instruction for the young, one would be ill advised indeed to ignore what is known about growth, its constraints and opportunities. And a theory of instruction—and this book is a series of exercises in such a theory—is in effect a theory of how growth and development are assisted by diverse means.

It is appropriate, then, that we begin with the problem of growth and its patterns. The subject is not yet well understood by any means, but it is plain that there is emerging a new consortium of disciplines that one day will constitute "the growth sciences," all of those fields concerned with understanding and facilitating the processes whereby human beings go so swiftly from a state of utter helplessness to one of control, what to our forebears would surely seem like fantastic control, of the environment.

The growth sciences will surely not "stop at the skin," and for reasons that are abundantly clear: man as a species, without culture, might in time reinvent the language and the technology that make possible the expression of his powers, but the growth of a "culturally naked" human being would be a very different picture indeed.

Each scientist approaches the problem from his own vantage point, and the vantage points are happily many. Perhaps it is well for me to begin somewhat autobiographically and trace the considerations that led me and various of my colleagues to get involved in the study of the development of such cognitive processes as problem solving, conceptualizing, thinking, perceptual recognition. After working on concept attainment—the strategies by which people discover equivalence in the things around them—I was enormously impressed at the logic-like or "rational" quality of adult human conceptualizing. While the conceptualizing efficiency of our subjects was not notably high—they wasted information in most unpuritan ways—nonetheless, they seemed to go about the task of searching for information in a manner that reflected recognition of complex environmental regularities, of their own limited capacities for processing information, of the risks involved in making certain kinds of guesses and choices of course. One could discern systematic strategies in behavior that had the quality and creases of well practiced rule-governed routines. The same could be said of the behavior of people whose processes of perceptual recognition I had studied for many years before and during the work on conceptualizing. Normal adult human beings not only use the minimal cues provided by split-second presentation of stimuli, but use them as a platform from which to leap to highly predictable conclusions. Much of perception involves going beyond the information given through reliance on a model of the world of events that makes possible interpolation, extrapolation, and prediction. Readiness in perception reflects not only the structure of the stimulus —its redundant features, to use a less ambiguous term—but also the likelihood of occurrence of events in a given context. Even when the context is stripped to a minimum, in the recognition of single words presented at brief exposures, the speed of recognition correlates within remarkably close limits with the likelihood of occurrence of those words in printed English. The Thorndike-Lorge *Word Book* has been a justified best-seller among students of perception!

It may well be that my astonishment at all this rational regularity was a reaction on my part to an earlier phase in which I had been deeply impressed by the role of motivational factors in perception. After all, affect and drive operated within quite narrow bounds both in perception and in thinking, and though "neurotic manifestations" or autism were everywhere evident, they did not operate in the processes of perceiving or thinking per se so much as in the way they prevented these processes from running their course. Even hospitalized psychotics could think, as witnessed by their excellent rationalizations and the closely woven structure of their delusions. My good friend and colleague Professor Gordon Allport was the one, of all people, who accused me at that juncture of being a rationalist. Perhaps it was the appearance of *A Study of Thinking*[1] that prompted him.

In any case, the next phase, after that book had appeared, was to inquire into the *origins* of human cognitive activity, and the result was the first of several false starts, all of which added together to give me some convictions about the proper study of intellectual development. That first start was motivated by a search for the irrational after a long Apollonian season. For two years, while starting other things as well, several of us carried out a study at the Judge Baker Guidance Center on the nature of "learning blocks" in children. We argued that just as pathological studies of brain damage had shed light on cognitive functioning, so too might studies of miscarried intellectual development shed light on the intellectual growth process. And so we had children in therapy and gave them special tutoring to help them over their scholastic difficulties.[2] We discovered one point of especial value for my own future inquiry. There is a sharp distinction that must be made between

[1] J. S. Bruner, J. J. Goodnow, and G. A. Austin, *A Study of Thinking* (New York: John Wiley & Sons, 1956).
[2] Our debt to Professor George Gardner, the Director of the Center, is very great.

behavior that *copes* with the requirements of a problem and behavior that is designed to *defend* against entry into the problem. It is the distinction one might make between playing tennis on the one hand and fighting like fury to stay off the tennis court altogether on the other. The latter is not a distorted version of the former; it is different activity, governed by a different objective and different requirements. The "distortion" in the learning activity of the unfortunate children we were studying and trying to help was not so much a distortion as it was the result of their working on a different set of problems from those the school had set for them. One could say the same thing about them that David Page has said about mathematics learning: when children give wrong answers it is not so often that they are wrong as that they are answering another question, and the job is to find out what question they are in fact answering. Once our blocked children were able to bear the problems as set—when we were able to give them a chance for conflict-free coping—their performance was quite like that of other children, although often less skilled since they had not quite learned to handle the technical instruments of the subjects they were supposed to be learning. The experience led us away from further studies of disturbed behavior, for our object has been to study how problems are dealt with and not how they are avoided. However valuable the topic of avoidance may be for an understanding of pathological processes, its study provides little information about the full range of growth. We would have floundered in studies of how children learn to avoid learning, which was not our intent (although I shall say more about it later). So I turned to work on the other end of the continuum—how people reach their high-water mark. This is how it came about that in a few years I found myself so deeply involved in educational matters.

With that much by way of background, let me grapple a little now with what is involved in intellectual growth. It is

easy enough to use one's chosen theory for explaining modifications in behavior as an instrument for describing growth; there
are so many aspects of growth that any theory can find something that it can explain well. Probably the best way to save
oneself from burrowing tunnels into the subject is to set up
some benchmarks about the nature of intellectual growth
against which to measure one's efforts at explanation. My own
list would include the following:

1. *Growth is characterized by increasing independence of
response from the immediate nature of the stimulus.* Much of
what the young child does is predictable from a knowledge of
the stimuli that are impinging upon him at the time he responds
or just prior to that time. A great deal of growth consists of the
child's being able to maintain an invariant response in the face
of changing states of the stimulating environment or learning
to alter his response in the presence of an unchanging stimulus
environment. He gains his freedom from stimulus control
through mediating processes, as they have come to be called
in recent years, that transform the stimulus prior to response.
Some of these mediating processes require considerable delay
between stimulus and response. A theory of growth that does
not attempt an account of these mediating processes and of
the nature of the transformations they make possible is not very
interesting psychology.

2. *Growth depends upon internalizing events into a "storage
system" that corresponds to the environment.* It is this system
that makes possible the child's increasing ability to go beyond
the information encountered on a single occasion. He does this
by making predictions and extrapolations from his stored
model of the world.

3. *Intellectual growth involves an increasing capacity to
say to oneself and others, by means of words or symbols, what
one has done or what one will do.* This self-accounting or self-
consciousness permits a transition from merely orderly be-

havior to logical behavior, so called. It is the process that leads to the eventual recognition of logical necessity—the so-called analytic mode of the philosophers—and takes human beings beyond empirical adaptation.

4. *Intellectual development depends upon a systematic and contingent interaction between a tutor and a learner,* the tutor already being equipped with a wide range of previously invented techniques that he teaches the child. Though it is obvious to say that the child is born into a culture and formed by it, it is not plain how a psychological theory of cognitive development deals with this fact. Moreover, it is necessary to take account of the various systematic relations a culture provides for dealing with the tutor-tutee relationship—the family, special identification figures, teachers, heroes, and so forth.

5. *Teaching is vastly facilitated by the medium of language, which ends by being not only the medium for exchange but the instrument that the learner can then use himself in bringing order into the environment.* The nature of language and the functions it serves must be part of any theory of cognitive development.

6. *Intellectual development is marked by increasing capacity to deal with several alternatives simultaneously, to tend to several sequences during the same period of time, and to allocate time and attention in a manner appropriate to these multiple demands.* There is a great distance indeed between the one-track mind of the young child and the ten-year-old's ability to deal with an extraordinarily complex world.

That will do as a minimal list—or perhaps it is too long, for quite plainly several items on the list overlap. Let me now turn to some specific theoretical notions and to a few experiments to illustrate them to see what can be said about the issues we have described.

Let me first dispose of one matter, a central one in the theory of development. Unquestionably, the most impressive figure in the field of cognitive development today is Jean Piaget. We and the generations that follow us will be grateful for his pioneering work. Piaget, however, is often interpreted in the wrong way by those who think that his principal mission is psychological. It is not. It is epistemological. He is deeply concerned with the nature of knowledge per se, knowledge as it exists at different points in the development of the child. He is considerably less interested in the processes that make growth possible, and handles these by a portmanteau theory of equilibria and disequilibria—a cycle between accommodation to the environment and assimilation of the environment to an internal schema. It is not his rather easy conception of equilibrium-disequilibrium that has contributed to our understanding of growth. Rather, it is his brilliant formal description of the nature of the knowledge that children exhibit at each stage of development. These descriptions are couched in terms of the logical structure that informs children's solutions of problems, the logical presuppositions upon which their explanations and manipulations are based. What he has done is to write the implicit logical theory on which the child proceeds in dealing with intellectual tasks. There are, to be sure, faults in his formal descriptions that have been attacked by logicians and mathematicians, but this is neither here nor there. What is overwhelmingly important is the utility and power of his descriptive work. But in no sense does this formal description constitute an explanation or a psychological description of the processes of growth. The descriptive clarity, rather, poses the question for anybody who would deal with psychological explanation.

Let me give an example from a recent study carried on in our laboratory.[3] We studied children between the ages of four and eleven. They were given the task of saying which of a pair of beakers was fuller and which emptier. Children at all these

[3] See chapter 8 in J. S. Bruner, R. R. Olver, P. M. Greenfield, et al., *Studies in Cognitive Growth* (New York: John Wiley & Sons, 1966).

ages have no difficulty in giving an appropriate response to pairs of identical beakers, whether filled to the same level or to different levels. Now we present a pair of half-filled glasses of unequal volume. Identifying the glass of larger volume as A, we often find that a child will say that A is fuller than B and then go on to say that A is emptier than B. Or he will say that both are equally full, but A is emptier. This seemed extraordinary to us, for it seemed like such patent contradiction.

What was the more astonishing was that the proportion of errors that were contradictory made by children of four through nine increased with age, rather than decreasing as one might have expected. Indeed, with glasses of unequal volume, 27 percent of the errors among the fives were contradictions, 52 percent among the sixes, and 68 percent among the sevens. What accounts for this astonishing increase in logical contradiction—calling something fuller and then saying it is emptier, or saying that two vessels are equally full and then claiming that one is emptier? There are two alternatives. The first is that older children are less logical, less concerned with consistency —which certainly seems far-fetched in the light of what else we know about intellectual growth between the ages of four and eleven. The other is that *logical* contradiction is not the issue at all, that it is a by-product of some other psychological process—perhaps of the way children go about defining and judging fullness and emptiness.

A look at how judgments are made quickly confirms the latter view. All the children in the age range we have studied judge fullness in about the same way, using a direct method of observing rather than the indirect method of computing proportion. That glass is judged fuller that has the greater apparent volume of water; and the favored indication of greater volume is water level, or, where water level is equated, then width of glass, or when width and water level are the same, then height of glass. All are criteria that can be pointed at. But now consider the judgments made by the different-aged children with respect to which glass in each pair is emptier. The older children have developed an interesting consistency based on an appreciation of the complementary relation of filled and empty space—albeit an incorrect one. For them "emptier" means the glass that has the largest volume of unfilled space, just as "fuller" meant the glass that had the largest volume of filled space. Good. But, in consequence, their responses seem logically contradictory. For the glass that is judged fuller also turns out to be the glass that is judged emptier—given a large glass and a small glass, both half full. The younger children, on the other hand, equate emptiness with liquid "littleness": that glass is emptier that gives the impression of being smaller in volume of liquid. So they end by being consistent in their judgments of fullness and emptiness.

What is interesting psychologically in the performance of these children is not the logical property of their reactions. Rather it is the development of a greater subtlety in the responses of the older children. The younger children are using a single criterion, apparent volume of water, in judging fullness and emptiness: more water = fuller, less water = emptier. It is a good rule of thumb, and it works for most pairs of glasses that are within range of each other in size. But note what the older children are doing. They have begun to dissociate two variables—empty space and full space—and while they cannot handle the two consistently by the yardstick of external logic, they can at least deal with them separately. The fact of the matter is that because they are still limited to definitions that are based upon pointing—call them ostensive definitions if you wish—they cannot yet handle the two variables by the use of proportion; what is intriguing about proportion is that it cannot be pointed at since it is a relation of two variables.

The logical account, then, tells little about the psychological development, though it surely helps in the description of the knowledge the children possess. We know from further research, for example, that the step of dissociating full space and empty space soon leads the child to consider the relationship between them; then by age ten the idea of proportion proper is born, thanks not to logic but to the abandonment of the need for pointing to a perceptual indication of each idea.

We can surely learn a lesson from this little experiment beyond the critique of logical description as a means of explicating the nature of intellectual growth. What does it mean that the child is limited in defining things by having to point at the defining properties of his ideas? And by what means does he come to dissociate different aspects of something like a glass into "empty space" and "filled space"? These are questions that lead us back to our benchmarks.

Take our first and second benchmarks, the question of representation: how the child gets free of present stimuli and conserves past experience in a model, and the rules that govern storage and retrieval of information from this model. Much of our research has been directed at the elucidation of this matter. What is meant by representation? What does it mean to translate experience into a model of the world? Let me suggest that there are probably three ways in which human beings accomplish this feat. The first is through action. We know many things for which we have no imagery and no words, and they are very hard to teach to anybody by the use of either words or diagrams and pictures. If you have tried to coach somebody at tennis or skiing or to teach a child to ride a bike, you will have been struck by the wordlessness and the diagrammatic impotence of the teaching process. (I heard a sailing instructor a few years ago engage with two children in a shouting match about "getting the luff out of the main"; the children understood every single word, but the sentence made no contact with their muscles. It was a shocking performance, like much that goes on in school.) There is a second system of representation that depends upon visual or other sensory organization and upon the use of summarizing images. We may, as in an experiment by Mandler,[4] grope our way through a maze of toggle switches, and then at a certain point in overlearning, come to recognize a visualizable path or pattern. We have come to talk about the first form of representation as *enactive,* the second as *iconic.* Iconic representation is principally governed by principles of perceptual organization and by the economical transformations in perceptual organization that Attneave has described[5]—techniques for filling in, completing, extrapolating. Enactive representation is based, it seems, upon a learning of responses and forms of habituation.

Finally, there is representation in words or language. Its hallmark is that it is *symbolic* in nature, with certain features of symbolic systems that are only now coming to be understood. Symbols (words) are arbitrary (as Hockett puts it,[6] there is no analogy between the symbol and the thing, so that *whale* can stand for a very big creature and *microorganism* for a very small one), they are remote in reference, and they are almost always highly productive or generative in the sense that a language or any symbol system has rules for the formation and transformation of sentences that can turn reality over on its beam ends beyond what is possible through actions or images. A language, for example, permits us to introduce lawful syntactic transformations that make it easy and useful to approach declarative propositions about reality in a most striking way. We observe an event and encode it—the dog bit the man. From this utterance we can travel to a range of possible recodings—did the dog bite the man or did he not? If he had not,

[4] G. Mandler, "From Association to Structure," *Psychological Review,* 69:415–427 (1962).

[5] F. Attneave, "Some Informational Aspects of Visual Perception," *Psychological Review,* 61:183–193 (1954).

[6] C. F. Hockett, "Animal 'Languages' and Human Language," in J. N. Spuhler, ed., *The Evolution of Man's Capacity for Culture* (Detroit: Wayne State University Press, 1959), pp. 32–39.

what would have happened? and so on. Grammar also permits us an orderly way of stating hypothetical propositions that may have nothing to do with reality—"The unicorn is in the garden"; "I speak a triangle, a mystery"; "In the beginning was the word."

I should also mention one other property of a symbolic system—its compactibility—a property that permits condensations of the order $F = MA$ or $S = \frac{1}{2}gt^2$ or "Gray is all theory / Green grows the golden tree of life," in each case the grammar being quite ordinary, though the semantic squeeze is enormous. My colleague George Miller has proposed a magic number 7 ± 2 as the range of human attention or immediate memory.[7] We are indeed limited in our span. Let me only suggest here that compacting or condensing is the means whereby we fill our seven slots with gold rather than dross.

What is abidingly interesting about the nature of intellectual development is that it seems to run the course of these three systems of representation until the human being is able to command all three.

In earliest childhood events and objects are defined in terms of the actions taken toward them. One is reminded of the James-Lange theory of emotions, according to which you feel frightened because you flee. An object is what one does to it. Piaget's classic demonstration of the growth of the idea of the permanent object is still the best: a one-year-old child, presented with a favorite toy, will not cry upon its removal unless he is holding it in his hand. Later, removal will bring tears if he has begun to move his hand out to reach it. Still later, it suffices to enrage him that it is removed when his eye has fallen on it. Finally, he will cry when the object, placed under a cover some time ago, is found to be missing when he returns to it.

---

[7] George Miller, "The Magical Number 7, Plus or Minus 2: Some Limits on Our Capacity for Processing Information," *Psychological Review,* 63:81–97 (1956).

Objects, in short, develop an autonomy that is not dependent upon action. If at first "a rattle is to shake" and "a hole is to dig," later they are somehow picturable or conceivable without action.

What appears next in development is a great achievement. Images develop an autonomous status, they become great summarizers of action. By age three the child has become a paragon of sensory distractibility. He is victim of the laws of vividness, and his action pattern is a series of encounters with this bright thing which is then replaced by that chromatically splendid one, which in turn gives way to the next noisy one. And so it goes. Visual memory at this stage seems to be highly concrete and specific. What is intriguing about this period is that the child is a creature of the moment; the image of the moment is sufficient and it is controlled by a single feature of the situation. The child can reproduce things that were there before—in the form that was there before. He can reproduce a pattern of nine glasses laid out in rows and columns with diameter and height varying systematically. Indeed, he does it as well as a seven-year-old. But he can only reproduce the order as he saw it—say with height increasing from left to right and diameter from top to bottom. The likeness of equivalent patterns (for instance, with diameter varying from left to right) is lost on the younger child. He can copy but not transpose.[8]

Or take the five-year-old, faced with two equal beakers, each filled to the same level with water. He will say that they are equal. Now pour the contents of one of the beakers into another that is taller and thinner and ask whether there is the same amount to drink in both. The child will deny it, pointing out that one of them has more because the water is higher. This incapacity to recognize invariance of magnitude across transformations in the appearance of things is one of the most striking aspects of this stage.

[8] See *Studies in Cognitive Growth,* chapter 7.

What makes the difference? I would like to suggest that it is the formation of the third or symbolic system of representation, based upon the translation of experience into language. But it is obviously not language per se that makes the difference; rather, it seems to be the use of language as an instrument of thinking that matters, its internalization, to use an apt but puzzling word. The very young child uses language almost as an extension of pointing, and recent work shows that the likelihood of a word's use in the early linguistic career of the child is vastly increased if the object is either in hand or in direct sight. It is only gradually that words are used to stand for objects not present, and it is a still longer time before such remote referring words are manipulated by the transformational apparatus of grammar in a manner designed to aid the solution of mental problems—tasks requiring that a barrier be overcome. And it is even later that words become the vehicle for dealing in the categories of the possible, the conditional, the counterfactual conditional, and in the rest of the vast realm of mind in which words and utterances have no direct referent at all in immediate experience. Yet it is in these realms that powerful representations of the world of possible experience are constructed and used as search models in problem solving.

How the transitions are effected—from enactive representation to iconic, and from both of these to symbolic—is a moot and troubled question. To put the matter very briefly, it would seem as if some sort of image formation or schema formation —whatever we should call the device that renders a sequence of action simultaneous, renders it into an immediate representation—comes rather automatically as an accompaniment of response stabilization. But how the nervous system converts a sequence of responses into an image or schema is simply not understood.

As for the internalization of language as an instrument of

thought—and we shall examine some of its effects on behavior in a moment—I think that a first step toward an answer has been proposed by Roger Brown and his colleagues.[9] I refer to their observations on early language learning, on the interchange between child and tutor, in which the child makes an utterance in his particular grammatical form, the tutor expands and idealizes the child's utterance into adult grammatical form, and the child then matches his utterance selectively to the adult model. The observations are confined principally to the second and third years of life. I would like to suggest that some extension of this process goes on throughout childhood—with parents, teachers, older children. It is less obvious, perhaps, but just as ubiquitous, and consists of a formational and transformational exchange. "I want the cake," "You can have it *after* [or *if*] you finish your egg." "I finished my egg now." And so on. I rather suspect that part of this more extended contingent dialogue relates to the learning of the small words—*if, to, from, above*, and the like. These, of course, are the last words that the child masters in acquiring adult speech, and they are the words that are crucial for converting complex experience and complex expectancy into a form that makes internal review possible.

Perhaps the most striking illustration of the difference between words and images as ways or reckoning with experience is illustrated by another experiment carried out at Harvard.[10] The children were from four to seven years old. The experiment was based on a novel argument. It was this. If the child customarily deals with things in terms of their image properties, though he may in fact have the language necessary to deal with them in a more powerful linguistic way, it must be

[9] R. W. Brown, C. Fraser, Ursula Bellugi, "Explorations in Grammar evaluations," in U. Bellugi and R. Brown, eds., *The Acquisition of Language*, Monographs of the Society for Research in Child Development, 29 (Chicago: University of Chicago Press, 1964), pp. 79–92.

[10] See *Studies in Cognitive Growth*, chapter 9.

that reckoning by the appearance of things inhibits his use of linguistic categories for dealing with the situation. For example, in the conservation experiment, the practiced tendency to consider the "higher" water level as more to drink may be so habitual and automatic as to prevent the child from employing more powerful means of analysis. If this is so, then one should get a marked improvement in performance by having the child work the problem out first "in his head" before ever seeing the displays, permitting linguistic or symbolic representation before the iconic mode can monopolize the situation. This was done. A screen was placed before the two glasses, covering all but their tops. The one standard glass was poured into the other behind the screen. The children were asked whether there was the same amount to drink in the hidden glass. Having made their judgments with the screen there, they were then presented with the glasses directly, with screen removed. What now: more, less, or same? Half of the four-year-olds and virtually all of the others say, when the screen is used, that the amount of water will be the same. Virtually no fours or fives say this in experiments with no screen present, and only about half of the sixes and sevens. When unscreening takes place and they are again confronted with the world of objects, the fours go right back. But not the others. They stick to their more sophisticated linguistic version. But note their explanations. "It looks different, but it really isn't." Or "It doesn't change when you only pour it." Language provides the means of getting free of immediate appearance as the sole basis of judgment.

Let me say one more thing about language in order to make the account complete. We have studied in very considerable detail the manner in which children impute similarity to things in their environment—how things may be called alike.[11] Between ages three and twelve, the child is learning to create

[11] See *Studies in Cognitive Growth,* chapter 2.

rules of equivalence that join together a set of objects by
what logicians speak of as a superordinate rule: that things
may be considered alike because *all* of them exhibit a common
characteristic. Before that, equivalence is not the true equivalence of the adult. Banana, peach, potato, milk, are eventually
all alike because they are all for eating, for example. But
before that, banana and peach were alike because they are
both yellow, peach and potato both have skins, peach and
potato and milk I had for lunch yesterday. They are fan-
tastically complicated rules in the sense that if you gave
them to a computer, following them would demand very
considerable memory and processing capacity. All such rules
deal with local likeness in appearance. The passage to sub-
ordinate grouping provides a kind of freedom from the immediacy of local similarities. This parallels the growth of the
distinction in the child's thought between appearance and
reality just mentioned. It is also paralleled by a shift in strategies for acquiring information. We play Twenty Questions
games with children. Up to the point when they master the
superordinate rule of equivalence, the typical question of
children is a direct test of an hypothesis. Indirect, constraining
questions aimed at narrowing the domain of possibilities are
rarely asked. To a young child, a question is an instrument
for obtaining information that can be pointed at as a cause:
"A car went off the road and hit a tree. What happened?"
"Did somebody bump him off the road?" "Did the driver
get stung by a bee?" The superordinate rule provides the way
of cumulating information, a way of dealing with longer
chains of inference. A thing now is not only *this* thing, but
a member of a larger class, and that is a member of a still
larger class, and so forth.

Let me return again and finally to the benchmarks of
intellectual growth with which we started. With respect to the
first of them, increasing independence of response from the

immediate environment, I think that we have only begun to
understand the representations that are used as mediators. Let
me lapse back into the autobiographical vein here. I have
always had difficulty with theories of stimulus-response con-
ditioning, whether based upon the idea of contiguity or of
reinforcement as the forger of links between stimuli and
responses. Accounting for the increasing freedom of behavior
from immediate stimulus control by interposing little invisible
s's and little r's between the stimulus and the final response
strikes me as futile. I'm inclined now to think that pure
stimulus-response theory may be a fairly adequate account
of the way learning takes place when the learner is operating
with enactive representation—either as a small infant or rendered into the posture of the small infant by the psychologist's
ingenious experimental apparatus that prevents anything from
happening but an overt response. I note with interest that
the Russians, having forsaken Pavlov's as their sole model
of learning and growth, have gone all the way to a second-
signal system that is based on the mediation of language
between stimulus and response. I think they are on the right
track, if their object is to go beyond infant learning.

Gestalt theory is the system par excellence for analysis
of the iconic mode, being solidly based upon the analysis of
the naive phenomenology of experience and the manner in
which perception and memory are linked by the rule of
phenomenal similarity. Much of the work of the now old New
Look in perception was directed similarly to the iconic mode.
Affective and motivational factors affect imagery and perceptual organization strikingly, particularly when impoverished
stimulus material is used and linguistic categorization rendered
ambiguous.

The persistently rational quality of behavior to which I
referred earlier enters the picture when there is internalization
of symbolic techniques—language in its natural form, and

then the artificial languages of number and logic. But there are various ways of processing information, and the symbolic mode is only one. Let me utter the suspicion that much of the intrusive nonrationality about us, the disruptive forms as well as powerful ones such as the metaphors of poetry, derives from our iconic and enactive operations upon experience.

Consider the dependence of growth upon a contingent tutor-learner interaction, and the failure of growth when this is absent. We know little about it, save in extreme cases where there has been real deprivation of contact between the child and adults. With Socrates, we know somehow that a dialogue can lead people to discover things of great depth and wisdom. What a pity we know so little of learning by dialogue save that the slave boy must have had home practice to have bene-fited from Socrates. He could not, to use our current term, have been culturally deprived. Vygotsky[12] and George Herbert Mead[13] have both suggested that later thought is often an internal version of this art of dialogue. There are even inventions that help, as in the dialogue between the thinker and his written words pondered later. In such reflection, notation of one sort or another surely becomes enormously important, whether by models, pictures, words, or mathematical symbols. Again there is a gap, and we know too little about the use of the notebook, the sketch, the outline, in reflective work.

Surely, the more we know about properties of language and its powers the more we shall know about the manner in which it can aid thought. There has been perhaps too much emphasis on the so-called Whorfian hypothesis—that different languages structure reality differently for their users. Much more to the point is the general question of how language as such affects

[12] L. S. Vygotsky, *Thought and Language,* ed. and trans. by Eugenia Hanfmann and Gertrude Vakar (New York: John Wiley and Sons, 1962).
[13] G. H. Mead, *Mind, Self, and Society* (Chicago: University of Chicago Press, 1934).

the cognitive processes, no matter what language. The new emphasis on language universals suggests a good starting place: what are the consequences that follow for thought from the most general properties of language? It is this concern that leads me to put language at the center of the stage in considering the nature of intellectual development.

Increasing capacity to attend to multiple aspects of the environment and to track several sequences at a time—both are partly dependent upon the nature of representation by the child to bring order into his world. Does attentional capacity grow? Do we develop more sheer strength in immediate memory? Or is it simply that these things are constant and we develop representational techniques such that the magic number 7 ± 2 is filled with purer and purer gold? I confess to a secret conviction that there are treasures to be found in understanding the means whereby children get over their distractibility and their overwhelming tendency to deal with one feature of the environment at a time.

Finally the matter of the development of self-accounting that permits the growing child to go from adaptive behavior to the self-conscious use of logic and reasoning. Let me focus on the idea of logical necessity. It seems reasonable to suppose that the idea of logical necessity depends upon a process of dealing not with experience directly but, as Piaget has put it, with the nature of propositions themselves. For it is in this way that we go beyond the empirical properties of concrete events, just as mathematicians operate upon the language rather than upon what the language refers to. It is the difference between treating symbols as if they were transparent and treating them as if they were opaque, for themselves and only with respect to themselves. The notion of logical necessity is somewhere in between what an unselfconscious child does and what a mathematician does. We develop a belief that there is a correspondence between the form of the proposition and the nature of events. *A* is greater than *B*, *B* greater than *C,* and therefore *A* is greater than *C,* because, in Peirce's pragmatic sense, it works in nature. I rather suspect it is a big step from there to the concern with the ordering of symbols in and of themselves, as in pure mathematics, logic, or linguistics. In any case, what I am urging is that one source of self-consciousness in intellectual development consists of an awareness of the notation in terms of which we have encoded experience.

Let me conclude with one last point. What I have said suggests that mental growth is in very considerable measure dependent upon growth from the outside in—a mastering of techniques that are embodied in the culture and that are passed on in a contingent dialogue by agents of the culture. This becomes notably the case when language and the symbolic systems of the culture are involved, for there are a multitude of models available in the culture for shaping symbolic usage —mentors of all shapes and conditions. I suspect that much of growth starts out by our turning around on our own traces and recoding in new forms, with the aid of adult tutors, what we have been doing or seeing, then going on to new modes of organization with the new products that have been formed by these recodings. We say, "I see what I'm doing now," or "So that's what the thing is." The new models are formed in increasingly powerful representational systems. It is this that leads me to think that the heart of the educational process consists of providing aids and dialogues for translating experience into more powerful systems of notation and ordering. And it is for this reason that I think a theory of development must be linked both to a theory of knowledge and to a theory of instruction, or be doomed to triviality.

Chapter 2

Education
as
Social Invention

I SHALL TAKE it as self-evident that each generation must define afresh the nature, direction, and aims of education to assure such freedom and rationality as can be attained for a future generation. For there are changes both in circumstances and in knowledge that impose constraints on and give opportunities to the teacher in each succeeding generation. It is in this sense that education is in constant process of invention. I should like particularly to comment upon four changes in our own time that require consideration in thinking about education.

The first of these derives from our increasing understanding of man as a species. As one reads the enormously rich reports of the last decade or two, it is plain that there has been a revolution that forces us to reconsider what it is we do when we occupy man's long growing period in certain ways now familiar as "schooling."

A second basis for redefining education is the increase in our understanding of the nature of individual mental growth. There have been profound reorientations in developmental theory in the last generation, changes that have been hastened by studies of normal and pathological growth, by analyses of the effects of different types of early environments, by studies of the development of language and its impact on thought. All of this work has forced us to reconsider the role of man's symbolic operations.

Third, there is reason to believe that we have come to understand the process of education somewhat more clearly than before. This has been a decade of intense educational experiment involving many of the finest minds of our generation. It has given me pause to see in what measure an eight-year-old can be led to grasp what a poem is, or come to a conception of the conservation of momentum, or arrive slowly but surely at the powerful generality of a quadratic function as a set of sets in which the elements in each set are the same as the number of sets.

Finally, and most obviously, the rate of change in the society in which we live forces us to redefine how we shall educate a new generation. John Dewey's *My Pedagogic Creed,* a movingly concerned document, rests principally upon reflections of the author prior to the first Great War—a yearningly long time ago.

I shall consider each of these matters; but before I do, I must confess some of my own doubts. It is reasonably plain to me, as a psychologist, that however able psychologists may be, it is not their function to decide upon educational goals any more than the ablest general decides whether a nation should or should not be at war. Whatever I know about policy-making reinforces the conviction that technicians and scientists often lack the kind of follow-up commitment that is the requisite of wise social policy. I cannot work up much enthusiasm for philosopher kings, psychologist kings, doctor kings, or even mixed-committee kings. The political process—and decisions about the aims of education must work their way through that process—is slow, perhaps, but is committed to the patient pursuit of the possible.

Yet it is also clear that generals do in fact have a strong

influence on the politics of war and peace and that scientists have had and will have a powerful influence on our defense and other policies. What is not so clear is the distinction between ends and means, between goals and their implementation. And perhaps it is just as well, for there is an intuitive familiarity that generals have with what is possible and what is not possible in war and in containing its threat, and there is a certain familiarity that psychologists have with how one can get somebody to learn or to pay attention or to stay free of anxiety. While these are not ends in the strict sense, they shape our ends in educational policy as in defense policy. It is, if you will, the psychologist's lively sense of what is possible that can make him a powerful force. If he fails to fill his role as a diviner and delineator of the possible, then he does not serve the society wisely. If he confuses his function and narrows his vision of the possible to what he counts as desirable, then we shall all be the poorer. He can and must provide the full range of alternatives to challenge the society to choice. And now back to the main theme.

How evaluate education in the light of our newly gained knowledge of man as a species? Let me begin by proposing a view that might best be called evolutionary instrumentalism. Man's use of mind is dependent upon his ability to develop and use "tools" or "instruments" or "technologies" that make it possible for him to express and amplify his powers. His very evolution as a species speaks to this point. It was consequent upon the development of bipedalism and the use of spontaneous pebble tools that man's brain and particularly his cortex developed. It was not a large-brained hominid that developed the technical-social life of the human; rather it was the tool-using, cooperative pattern that gradually changed man's morphology by favoring the survival of those who could link themselves with tool systems and disfavoring those who tried to go it on big jaws, heavy dentition, or superior weight. What evolved as a human nervous system was something, then, that required outside devices for expressing its potential. It was a swift progress. The first primitive primates appeared five million years ago and man reached his present morphology and brain size about half a million years ago—with the major development of higher hominid to tool-user occupying probably less than half a million of the years between. From then on, all major changes in the species were, in Weston La Barre's startling phrase, by prosthetic devices,[1] by man's learning how to link himself to amplifiers of his muscles, of his senses, and of his powers of ratiocination.

The British biologist Peter Medawar remarks that it is likely that at about this same point in human history human culture became sufficiently elaborated for evolution to become Lamarckian and reversible rather than Darwinian and irreversible.[2] It is a figure of speech, of course, but Medawar's point is well taken: what is transmitted by the culture is indeed a pool of acquired characteristics, a pool that can get lost just as surely as the Easter Islanders, the Incas, and the Mayans lost whatever skills made it possible for them to leave such splendid ruins to disabled descendants whose genes were probably not one whit changed.

I know that the terms "tool" and "technology" and even "instrument" offend when one speaks of man as dependent upon them for the realization of his humanity. For these words denote "hardware," and it is mostly "software" that I have in mind—skills that are tools. Language is perhaps the ideal example of one such powerful technology, with its power not only for communication but for encoding "reality," for

[1] Weston La Barre, *The Human Animal* (Chicago: University of Chicago Press, 1954).
[2] Peter Medawar, "Onwards from Spencer: Evolution and Evolutionism," *Encounter* 21(3):35–43 (September 1963).

representing matters remote as well as immediate, and for doing all these things according to rules that permit us both to represent "reality" and to transform it by conventional yet appropriate rules. All of this depends on the external resources of a grammar, a lexicon, and (likely as not) a supporting cast of speakers constituting the linguistic community.

Language happens to be a tool of the most general sort, in the sense that it provides direction and amplification for the way we use our muscular apparatus, our senses, and our powers of reflection. But each of these domains also has its skills that are expressed through various kinds of tool-using. There are time- and strength-saving skills for using our muscles, and they are built into the tools we devise for them. There are attention-saving skills in perception that are imparted and then become the basis for understanding the icons we construct for representing things by drawing, diagram, and design. And there are, finally and most importantly, strain-reducing heuristics to help us figure out things—how to cancel out nuisance parameters, how to use our heads and save our heels, how to make quick but decent approximations, and so on.

Many of these skills are taught in the subtle interaction of parent and child—as in the case of primary linguistic skills. And, as in the case of language learning, where the pedagogy is highly unselfconscious, it is probably true that most of the primitive skills of manipulating and looking and attending are also taught in this way. It is when the society goes beyond these relatively primitive techniques that the less spontaneous instruction of school must be relied upon. At this point the culture necessarily comes to rely upon its formal education as a means of providing skills. And insofar as there has been any innovation in tools or tool-using (taking these expressions in the broadest sense), the educational system is the sole means of dissemination—the sole agent of evolution, if you will.

Consider now our understanding of the nature of human ontogenetic development. Several important conclusions stand out. None of them, so far as I know, have been seriously considered in defining the aims and conduct of education.

The first is that mental growth is not a gradual accretion, either of associations or of stimulus-response connections or of means-end readinesses or of anything else. It appears to be much more like a staircase with rather sharp risers, more a matter of spurts and rests. The spurts ahead in growth seem to be touched off when certain capacities begin to develop. And some capacities must be matured and nurtured before others can be called into being. The sequence of their appearance is highly constrained. But these steps or stages or spurts or whatever you may choose to call them are *not* very clearly linked to age: some environments can slow the sequence down or bring it to a halt, others move it along faster. In the main, one can characterize these constrained sequences as a series of prerequisites. It is not until the child can hold in mind two features of a display at once, for example, that he can deal with their relationship, as in a ratio.

The steps or stages have been variously described by a variety of investigators working in centers as various as Geneva, Moscow, Paris, London, Montreal, Chicago, and Cambridge, but they seem to have an interesting likeness, even though the proposed dynamism varies. The first stages are relatively manipulative, marked by highly unstable and single-track attention. Knowing is principally knowing how to do, and there is minimum reflection. There follows a period of more reflective functioning in which the young human being is capable of an internal representation, by representative images, of greater chunks of the environment. The high point in this stage is between five and seven. Finally, something very special happens around adolescence, when language becomes increasingly important as a medium of thought. It is

evidenced by an ability to consider propositions rather than
objects; concepts become more exclusively hierarchal in structure; alternative possibilities can be handled in a combinatorial fashion. There is considerable doubt whether these
things have anything directly to do with the onset of physi-
ological adolescence—for there are equally sharp cognitive
turning points at the onset of language and at the age five-to-
seven turning point without much discernible assist from
hormonal tides. And hormonal adolescents in technically less
mature societies do not enter this stage.

What comes out of this picture, rough though I have
sketched it, is a view of human beings who have developed
three parallel systems for processing information and for
representing it—one through manipulation and action, one
through perceptual organization and imagery, and one through
symbolic apparatus. It is not that these are "stages" in any
sense; they are rather emphases in development. You must get
the perceptual field organized around your own person as
center before you can impose other, less egocentric axes upon
it, for example. In the end, the mature organism seems to
have gone through a process of elaborating three systems of
skills that correspond to the three major tool systems to which
he must link himself for full expression of his capacities—
tools for the hand, for the distance receptors, and for the
process of reflection.

It is not surprising in the light of this that early opportunities
for development have loomed so large in our recent understanding of human mental growth. The importance of early
experience is only dimly sensed today. The evidence from
animal studies indicates that virtually irreversible deficits can
be produced in mammals by depriving them of opportunities
that challenge their nascent capacities. In the last few years
there have been reports showing the crippling effect of deprived
human environments, as well as indications that "replacement

therapies" can be of considerable success, even at an age on the edge of adolescence. The principal deficits appear to be linguistic in the broadest sense—the lack of opportunity to share in dialogue, to have occasion for paraphrase, to internalize speech as a vehicle of thought. None of these matters are well understood, save that the principle discussed earlier seems to be operative, that, unless certain basic skills are mastered, later, more elaborated ones become increasingly out of reach. It is in the light of this fact that we can understand the increasing difference of intelligence with age between such culturally deprived groups as rural Southern Negroes and more culturally privileged whites. In time, and with sufficient failure, the gap is reinforced to irreversibility by a sense of defeat.

What has been learned about the educational process that may give guidance to our task of redefinition? Very little that is certain, but some extremely interesting impressions that can possibly be converted into testable hypotheses.

The "curriculum revolution" has made it plain even after only a decade that the idea of "readiness" is a mischievous half-truth. It is a half-truth largely because it turns out that one *teaches* readiness or provides opportunities for its nurture, one does not simply wait for it. Readiness, in these terms, consists of mastery of those simpler skills that permit one to reach higher skills. Readiness for Euclidian geometry can be gained by teaching intuitive geometry or by giving children an opportunity to build increasingly elaborate constructions with polygons. Or, to take the aim of the new, "second-generation" mathematics project,[3] if you wish to teach the calculus in the eighth grade, then begin it in the first grade by teaching the kinds of ideas and skills necessary for its mastery later.

[3] See the report of the Cambridge Conference on School Mathematics, *Goals for School Mathematics* (Boston: Houghton Mifflin, 1963).

Mathematics is no exception to the general rule, though admittedly it is the most easily understood from the point of view of what must be clear before something else can be grasped. Since most subjects can be translated into forms that place emphasis upon doing, or upon the development of appropriate imagery, or upon symbolic-verbal encoding, it is often possible to render the end result to be achieved in a simpler, more manageable form so that the child can move more easily and deeply to full mastery.

The second thing that emerges from pedagogical experiments of the last decade is that cognitive or intellectual mastery is rewarding. It is particularly so when the learner recognizes the cumulative power of learning, that learning one thing permits him to go on to something that before was out of reach, and so on toward such perfection as one may reach. It is a truth that every good athletic coach since the Greek Olympics has known. Teachers also gain pleasure when a student learns to recognize his own progress well enough so that he can take over as his own source of reward and punishment.

A third result of contemporary exploration in teaching is the conclusion that educational experiment, in the main, has been conducted and is being conducted in the dark—without feedback in usable form. The substitute for light (or usable feedback) is evaluation after the job has been completed. After the working party has been scattered, the evaluators enter. By then, it is so late in the day that only patching can be done. Indeed, such is the latitude in the choice of criteria for evaluation that something nice can usually be said about practically any course or curriculum. It would seem much more sensible to put evaluation into the picture *before and during* curriculum construction, as a form of intelligence operation to help the curriculum maker in his choice of material, in his approach, in his manner of setting tasks for the learner.

Finally, one is struck by the absence of a theory of instruction as a guide to pedagogy—a prescriptive theory on how to proceed in order to achieve various results, a theory that is neutral with respect to ends but exhaustive with respect to means. It is interesting that there is a lack of an integrating theory in pedagogy, that in its place there is principally a body of maxims.

As our technology grows increasingly complex in both machinery and human organization, the role of the school becomes more central in the society, not simply as an agent of socialization, but as a transmitter of basic skills. To this we turn next as our final basis for redefining education—the changing society.

In recent years I have wondered, particularly in connection with work in West Africa, why societies are not more mindful of the role of education in shaping their futures. Why in Africa, for example, is the short-term political allure of universal primary education given priority over training a corps of administrators, teachers, and technicians? In many cases, the second is financially precluded by the first, and the long-run result may prove a terrible time bomb as semiliterate youths flock into the new urban Africa with no marketable skills, their familial and tribal boats burned, and no properly trained corps of teachers and civil servants to maintain stability or to teach the untrained.

That is what set me brooding, and while I have no answer to the African problem, I do have some thoughts about our own. They crystallized while reading an essay by the distinguished Italian architect-designer Pier Luigi Nervi.[4] Nervi describes the loss in freedom of the architect-designer in an age

[4] Pier Luigi Nervi, "Is Architecture Moving Toward Forms and Characteristics Which Are Unchangeable?" in Gyorgy Kepes, ed., *Structure in Art and Science* (New York: Braziller, 1965).

of technological maturity. You can build a road or a path in any meandering shape you wish, provided the only users are men on foot, or on horse, or in wagons, or in slow cars. But the moment the speed of the vehicle passes a certain critical point, fantasy is constrained and you must conform to the idea of a containing arc. A car at seventy cannot turn on a fanciful curlicue.

There was a great deal of public soul-searching at the time of Sputnik as to whether our educational system was adequate to the task ahead. In fact, much new curriculum reform had started before then—out of a sense of the frightening gap between expert knowledge of our technology and public knowledge. I rather suspect that there will never again be such a period of careless or ritualistic regard for public education —but, then, universal public education as a working concept is not yet a century old!

It may well be the case that not only are we entering a period of technological maturity in which education will require constant redefinition, but that the period ahead may involve such a rapid rate of change in specific technology that narrow skills will become obsolete within a reasonably short time after their acquisition. Indeed, perhaps one of the defining properties of a highly matured technology is that there exists a lively likelihood of major technological change within the compass of a single generation—just as ours has seen several such major changes.

I entertained myself and some young students with whom I was working during the summer of 1964 on a social-studies curriculum by formulating Bruner's Rule—critical changes related to the order of magnitude in years away. I used this as an extension of the square law for the retinal angle—that the size of the retinal image is the reciprocal of the square of the distance of an object from the eye. Therefore, the further away a period of time, the longer its duration in order to be discerned! And so:

5×10^9	5,000,000,000	Birth of Earth
5×10^8	500,000,000	Vertebrates
5×10^7	50,000,000	Mammals
5×10^6	5,000,000	Primates
5×10^5	500,000	Present man
5×10^4	50,000	Great glacial migrations
5×10^3	5,000	Recorded history
5×10^2	500	Printing
5×10^1	50	Radio / mass education
5×10^0	5	Artificial intelligence

What I learned from my pupils was their conclusion that things were coming thick and fast. Life probably started about 2.5×10^9, so that half the history of the earth was lifeless. Some 99.999 percent of the earth's life has been manless, and from there on out the record is impressive and awesome. It would seem, indeed, as if the principal thing about tools and techniques is that they beget other more advanced ones at ever-increasing speed. And as the technology matures in this way, education in its very nature takes on an increasing role by providing the skills needed to manage and control the expanding enterprise.

The first response of educational systems under such acceleration is to produce technicians and engineers and scientists as needed, but it is doubtful whether such a priority produces what is required to manage the enterprise. For no specific science or technology provides a metalanguage in terms of which to think about a society, its technology, its science, and the constant changes that these undergo with innovation. Could an automotive engineer have foreseen the death of small-town America with the advent of the automobile? He would have been so wedded to his task of making better and better automobiles that it would never have occurred to him to consider the town, the footpath, leisure, or local loyalty. Somehow, if change is to be managed, it requires men with skills in sensing continuity and opportunity for continuity. This is a matter to which we shall return shortly.

What may we conclude from all this? It seems to me that four general policies follow from the issues that we have passed in review.

The first has to do with what is taught. It would seem, from our consideration of man's evolution, that principal emphasis in education should be placed upon skills—skills in handling, in seeing and imaging, and in symbolic operations, particularly as these relate to the technologies that have made them so powerful in their human expression.

It is hard to spell out in specific terms what such an emphasis upon skills entails, but some examples might provide a concrete basis for criticism. With respect, first, to the education of the perceptual-imaginal capacities, I can suggest at least one direction to travel. It is in the training of subtle spatial imagery. I have recently been struck by the increased visual power and subtlety of students exposed to courses in visual design—all differently conceived and with different objectives in view: one for undergraduates given by I. A. Richards at Harvard, another for teachers by Bartlett Hayes at Andover, and a third for city planners given by Gyorgy Kepes and Kevin Lynch at M.I.T. All of them produced what seemed to me like fresh discrimination in viewing the altered environment of urban America; all provided the students with new models in terms of which to analyze and sort their surroundings. My colleagues Gerald Holton and Edward Purcell have been experimenting with instruction in visual pattern as a mode of increasing the visualizing subtlety of concentrators in physics—visual subtlety and capacity to represent events visually and nonmetrically. I do not think that we have begun to scratch the surface of training in visualization—whether related to the arts, to science, or simply to the pleasures of viewing our environments more richly. Let me note in passing, by the way, that Maria Montessori, that strange blend of the mystic and the pragmatist, was groping toward some such conception as this.

At the level of symbolic operation, I think the work of Martin Deutsch with underprivileged children provides an interesting case in point—a conscious effort to lead children to verbal skills, to a sense of paraphrase and exchange.[5] It surely should not be limited, such an effort, to the under-privileged. The new mathematics curricula illustrate how much can be done in training symbolic skills.

This brings us immediately to a second conclusion. It relates literally to the meaning of the word *curriculum,* a word that derives from a course to be run. It is perhaps a wrong word. A curriculum should involve the mastery of skills that in turn lead to the mastery of still more powerful ones, the establishment of self-reward sequences. It is clear that this can be done in mathematics and science. But it is also the case that reading simpler poetry brings more complex poetry into reach, or that reading a poem once makes a second reading more rewarding. The reward of deeper understanding is a more robust lure to effort than we have yet realized.

A corollary of this conclusion (one I have urged before) is that there is an appropriate version of any skill or knowledge that may be imparted at whatever age one wishes to begin teaching—however preparatory the version may be. The choice of the earlier version is based upon what it is one is hoping to cumulate. The deepening and enrichment of this earlier understanding is again a source of reward for intellectual labors.

The third conclusion relates to change. If there is any way of adjusting to change, it must include, as we have noted, the development of a metalanguage and "metaskills" for dealing with continuity in change. What these might be is, of course,

[5] Martin Deutsch, "The Disadvantaged Child and the Learning Process: Some Social Psychological and Developmental Considerations," in A. Harry Passow, ed., *Education in Depressed Areas* (New York: Teachers College Press, 1963).

a moot point, but not completely so by any means. Mathematics is surely the most general metalanguage we have developed, and it provides the forms and patterns in terms of which regularities in nature are comprehended. I find myself forced to the conclusion that our survival may one day depend upon achieving a requisite mathematical literacy for rendering the seeming shocks of change into something that is continuous and cumulative. But, by the same token, there is a second discipline that deals with the search for likeness beneath the surface of diversity and change. It is, of course, the discipline of poetry, the vehicle for searching out unsuspected kinship.

A further speculation about preparation for change is that we are bound to move toward instruction in the sciences of behavior and away from the study of history. Recorded history is only about five thousand years old, as we saw. Most of what we teach is within the last few centuries, for the records before that are minimal while the records after are relatively rich. But just suppose that the richness of record increases as a function of our ability to develop systems for storing and retrieving information. A thousand years from now we will be swamped. One would surely not dwell then with such loving care over the details of Brumaire or the Long Parliament or the Louisiana Purchase. These are the furbelows of documentary short supply. But there is a more compelling reason to shift away from history toward the social or behavioral sciences.

It has to do with the need for studying the possible rather than the achieved—a necessary step if we are to adapt to change. It is the behavioral sciences and their generality with respect to variations in the human condition that must be central to our presentation of man, not the particularities of his history. This is not to say that we should give up study of the past, but rather that we should pursue such study with a different end in view—the end of developing style. For the development of style, be it style of writing or loving or dancing or eating, requires a sense of contrast and concreteness, and this we do not find in the behavioral sciences.

Finally, it is plain that if we are to evolve freely as a species by the use of the instrument of education, then we shall have to bring far greater resources to bear in designing our educational system. For one thing, if we are to respond to accelerated change, then we shall have to reduce turn-around time in the system. To do this requires greater participation on the part of those at the frontiers of learning. A distinguished mathematician and teacher, John Kemeny, did a survey of high-school mathematics teaching a decade ago and found no mathematics newer than a hundred years old being taught! That has been remedied somewhat in the decade since, but the work has hardly begun.

Another resource that must be brought to bear is modern psychology. Something happened to educational psychology a few decades ago that brought it to the low status it now enjoys. The circumstances need not concern us save in one respect. Part of the failure of educational psychology was its failure to grasp the full scope of its mission. It has too readily assumed that its central task was the application of personality theory or of group dynamics or whatnot. In fact, none of these efforts produced a major contribution to educational practice largely because the task was not really one of application in any obvious sense, but of formulation. Learning theory, for example, is distilled from descriptions of behavior in situations where the environment has been arranged either for the convenience of observing learning behavior or out of a theoretical interest in some special aspect of learning—reinforcement, cue distinctiveness, or whatever. But a theory of instruction, which must be at the heart of educational psychology, is principally concerned with how to arrange environments to optimize learning according to various criteria—to optimize transfer or retrievability of information, for example. Psychologists must re-enter the field of education in order to contribute to man's further evolution, an evolution that now proceeds through social invention. For it is psychology more than any other discipline that has the tools for exploring the limits of man's perfectibility. By doing so, it can, I think, have its major social impact by keeping lively the society's full sense of what is possible.

Aside from that, it becomes necessary for the various fields of learning to assess the manner in which they contribute to the amplification of mind—the way of doing or experiencing or ratiocinating that is integral to them and that should be part of the way of mind of an educated member of the culture. There are too many particulars to teach and to master. If we are to do justice to our evolution, we shall need, as never before, a way of transmitting the crucial ideas and skills, the acquired characteristics that express and amplify man's powers. We may be sure that the task will demand our highest talents. I would be content if we began, all of us, by recognizing that this is our task as learned men and scientists, that discovering how to make something comprehensible to the young is only a continuation of making something comprehensible to ourselves in the first place—that understanding and aiding others to understand are both of a piece.

Chapter 3

Notes on
a Theory
of Instruction

IN THIS ESSAY I shall attempt to develop a few simple theorems about the nature of instruction. I shall try to illustrate them by reference to the teaching and learning of mathematics. The choice of mathematics as a mode of illustration is not premised on the typicality of mathematics, for mathematics is restricted to well-formed problems and does not concern itself with empirical proof by either experiment or observation. Nor is this an attempt to elucidate mathematical teaching as such, for that would be beyond my competence. Rather, mathematics offers an accessible and simple example for what, perforce, will be a simplified set of propositions about teaching and learning. And there are data available from mathematics learning that have some bearing on our problem.

The plan is as follows. First some characteristics of a theory of instruction will be set forth, followed by a statement of some highly general theorems about the instructional process. I shall then attempt, in the light of specific observations of mathematics learning, to convert these general propositions into workable hypotheses. In conclusion, some remarks will be made on the nature of research in support of curriculum making.

A theory of instruction is *prescriptive* in the sense that it sets forth rules concerning the most effective way of achieving knowledge or skill. By the same token, it provides a yardstick for criticizing or evaluating any particular way of teaching or learning.

A theory of instruction is a *normative* theory. It sets up criteria and states the conditions for meeting them. The criteria must have a high degree of generality: for example, a theory of instruction should not specify in *ad hoc* fashion the conditions for efficient learning of third-grade arithmetic; such conditions should be derivable from a more general view of mathematics learning.

One might ask why a theory of instruction is needed, since psychology already contains theories of learning and of development. But theories of learning and of development are descriptive rather than prescriptive. They tell us what happened after the fact: for example, that most children of six do not yet possess the notion of reversibility. A theory of instruction, on the other hand, might attempt to set forth the best means of leading the child toward the notion of reversibility. A theory of instruction, in short, is concerned with how what one wishes to teach can best be learned, with improving rather than describing learning.

This is not to say that learning and developmental theories are irrelevant to a theory of instruction. In fact, a theory of instruction must be concerned with both learning and development and must be congruent with those theories of learning and development to which it subscribes.

A theory of instruction has four major features.

First, a theory of instruction should specify the experiences which most effectively implant in the individual a predisposition toward learning—learning in general or a particular type of learning. For example, what sorts of relationships with people and things in the preschool environment will tend to make the child willing and able to learn when he enters school?

Second, a theory of instruction must specify the ways in which a body of knowledge should be structured so that it can be most readily grasped by the learner. "Optimal structure" refers to a set of propositions from which a larger body of knowledge can be generated, and it is characteristic that the formulation of such structure depends upon the state of advance of a particular field of knowledge. The nature of different optimal structures will be considered in more detail shortly. Here it suffices to say that since the merit of a structure depends upon its power for *simplifying information,* for *generating new propositions,* and for *increasing the manipulability of a body of knowledge,* structure must always be related to the status and gifts of the learner. Viewed in this way, the optimal structure of a body of knowledge is not absolute but relative.

Third, a theory of instruction should specify the most effective sequences in which to present the materials to be learned. Given, for example, that one wishes to teach the structure of modern physical theory, how does one proceed? Does one present concrete materials first in such a way as to elicit questions about recurrent regularities? Or does one begin with a formalized mathematical notation that makes it simpler to represent regularities later encountered? What results are in fact produced by each method? And how describe the ideal mix? The question of sequence will be treated in more detail later.

Finally, a theory of instruction should specify the nature and pacing of rewards and punishments in the process of learning and teaching. Intuitively it seems quite clear that as learning progresses there is a point at which it is better to shift away from extrinsic rewards, such as a teacher's praise, toward the intrinsic rewards inherent in solving a complex problem for oneself. So, too, there is a point at which immediate reward for performance should be replaced by deferred reward. The timing of the shift from extrinsic to intrinsic and from immediate to deferred reward is poorly understood and obviously important. Is it the case, for example, that wherever learning involves the integration of a long sequence of acts, the shift should be made as early as possible from immediate to deferred reward and from extrinsic to intrinsic reward?

It would be beyond the scope of a single essay to pursue in any detail all the four aspects of a theory of instruction set forth above. What I shall attempt to do here is to explore a major theorem concerning each of the four. The object is not comprehensiveness but illustration.

PREDISPOSITIONS

It has been customary, in discussing predispositions to learn, to focus upon cultural, motivational, and personal factors affecting the desire to learn and to undertake problem solving. For such factors are of deep importance. There is, for example, the relation of instructor to student—whatever the formal status of the instructor may be, whether teacher or parent. Since this is a relation between one who possesses something and one who does not, there is always a special problem of authority involved in the instructional situation. The regulation of this authority relationship affects the nature of the learning that occurs, the degree to which a learner develops an independent skill, the degree to which he is confident of his ability to perform on his own, and so on. The relations between one who instructs and one who is instructed is never indifferent in its effect upon learning. And since the instructional process is essentially social—particularly in its early stages when it involves at least a teacher and a pupil—it is clear that the child, especially if he is to cope with school, must have minimal mastery of the social skills necessary for engaging in the instructional process.

There are differing attitudes toward intellectual activity in different social classes, the two sexes, different age groups, and different ethnic groupings. These culturally transmitted attitudes also pattern the use of mind. Some cultural traditions are, by count, more successful than others in the production of scientists, scholars, and artists. Anthropology and psychology investigate the ways a "tradition" or "role" affects attitudes toward the use of mind. A theory of instruction concerns itself, rather, with the issue of how best to utilize a given cultural pattern in achieving particular instructional ends.

Indeed, such factors are of enormous importance. But we shall concentrate here on a more cognitive illustration: upon the predisposition to explore alternatives.

Since learning and problem solving depend upon the exploration of alternatives, instruction must facilitate and regulate the exploration of alternatives on the part of the learner.

There are three aspects to the exploration of alternatives, each of them related to the regulation of search behavior. They can be described in shorthand terms as *activation, maintenance,* and *direction.* To put it another way, exploration of alternatives requires something to get it started, something to keep it going, and something to keep it from being random.

The major condition for activating exploration of alternatives in a task is the presence of some optimal level of uncertainty. Curiosity, it has been persuasively argued,[1] is a response to uncertainty and ambiguity. A cut-and-dried routine task provokes little exploration; one that is too uncertain may arouse confusion and anxiety, with the effect of reducing exploration.

The maintenance of exploration, once it has been activated,

[1] D. E. Berlyne, *Conflict, Arousal, and Curiosity* (New York: McGraw-Hill, 1960).

requires that the benefits from exploring alternatives exceed the risks incurred. Learning something with the aid of an instructor should, if instruction is effective, be less dangerous or risky or painful than learning on one's own. That is to say, the consequences of error, of exploring wrong alternatives, should be rendered less grave under a regimen of instruction, and the yield from the exploration of correct alternatives should be correspondingly greater.

The appropriate direction of exploration depends upon two interacting considerations: a sense of the goal of a task and a knowledge of the relevance of tested alternatives to the achievement of that goal. For exploration to have direction, in short, the goal of the task must be known in some approximate fashion, and the testing of alternatives must yield information as to where one stands with respect to it. Put in briefest form, direction depends upon knowledge of the results of one's tests, and instruction should have an edge over "spontaneous" learning in providing more of such knowledge.

STRUCTURE AND THE FORM OF KNOWLEDGE

Any idea or problem or body of knowledge can be presented in a form simple enough so that any particular learner can understand it in a recognizable form.

The structure of any domain of knowledge may be characterized in three ways, each affecting the ability of any learner to master it: the *mode of representation* in which it is put, its *economy,* and its effective *power*. Mode, economy, and power vary in relation to different ages, to different "styles" among learners, and to different subject matters.

Any domain of knowledge (or any problem within that domain of knowledge) can be represented in three ways: by a set of actions appropriate for achieving a certain result (enactive representation); by a set of summary images or graphics that stand for a concept without defining it fully (iconic representation); and by a set of symbolic or logical propositions drawn from a symbolic system that is governed by rules or laws for forming and transforming propositions (symbolic representation). The distinction can most conveniently be made concretely in terms of a balance beam, for we shall have occasion later to consider the use of such an implement in teaching children quadratic functions. A quite young child can plainly act on the basis of the "principles" of a balance beam, and indicates that he can do so by being able to handle himself on a see-saw. He knows that to get his side to go down farther he has to move out farther from the center. A somewhat older child can represent the balance beam to himself either by a model on which rings can be hung and balanced or by a drawing. The "image" of the balance beam can be varyingly refined, with fewer and fewer irrelevant details present, as in the typical diagrams in an introductory textbook in physics. Finally, a balance beam can be described in ordinary English, without diagrammatic aids, or it can be even better described mathematically by reference to Newton's Law of Moments in inertial physics. Needless to say, actions, pictures, and symbols vary in difficulty and utility for people of different ages, different backgrounds, different styles. Moreover, a problem in the law would be hard to diagram; one in geography lends itself to imagery. Many subjects, such as mathematics, have alternative modes of representation.

Economy in representing a domain of knowledge relates to the amount of information that must be held in mind and processed to achieve comprehension. The more items of information one must carry to understand something or deal with a problem, the more successive steps one must take in processing that information to achieve a conclusion, and the less the economy. For any domain of knowledge, one can rank summaries of it in terms of their economy. It is more economical (though less powerful) to summarize the American Civil War as a "battle over slavery" than as "a struggle between an expanding industrial region and one built upon a class society for control of federal economic policy." It is more economical to summarize the characteristics of free-falling bodies by the formula $S = \frac{1}{2}gt^2$ than to put a series of numbers into tabular form summarizing a vast set of observations made on different bodies dropped different distances in different gravitational fields. The matter is perhaps best epitomized by two ways of imparting information, one requiring carriage of much information, the other more a pay-as-you-go type of information processing. A highly imbedded sentence is an example of the former (This is the squirrel that the dog that the girl that the man loved fed chased); the contrast case is more economical (This is the man that loved the girl that fed the dog that chased the squirrel).

Economy, as we shall see, varies with mode of representation. But economy is also a function of the sequence in which material is presented or the manner in which it is learned. The case can be exemplified as follows (I am indebted to Dr. J. Richard Hayes for this example). Suppose the domain of knowledge consists of available plane service within a twelve-hour period between five cities in the Northeast—Concord, New Hampshire, Albany, New York, Danbury, Connecticut, Elmira, New York, and Boston, Massachusetts. One of the ways in which the knowledge can be imparted is by asking the student to memorize the following list of connections:

Boston to Concord
Danbury to Concord
Albany to Boston
Concord to Elmira
Albany to Elmira
Concord to Danbury
Boston to Albany
Concord to Albany

Now we ask, "What is the shortest way to make a round trip from Albany to Danbury?" The amount of information processing required to answer this question under such conditions is considerable. We increase economy by "simplifying terms" in certain characteristic ways. One is to introduce an arbitrary but learned order—in this case, an alphabetical one. We rewrite the list:

> Albany to Boston
> Albany to Elmira
> Boston to Albany
> Boston to Concord
> Concord to Albany
> Concord to Danbury
> Concord to Elmira
> Danbury to Concord

Search then becomes easier, but there is still a somewhat trying sequential property to the task. Economy is further increased by using a diagrammatic notation, and again there are varying degrees of economy in such recourse to the iconic mode. Compare the diagram on the left and the one on the right.

The latter contains at a glance the information that there is only one way from Albany to Danbury and return, that Elmira is a "trap," and so on. What a difference between this diagram and the first list!

The effective power of any particular way of structuring a domain of knowledge for a particular learner refers to the generative value of *his* set of learned propositions. In the last paragraph, rote learning of a set of connections between cities resulted in a rather inert structure from which it was difficult to generate pathways through the set of cities. Or, to take an example from a recent work,[2] children who are told that "Mary is taller than Jane, and Betty is shorter than Jane" are often unable to say whether Mary is taller than Betty. One can perfectly well remark that the answer is "there" in the logic of transitivity. But to say this is to miss the psychological point. Effective power will, to be sure, never exceed the inherent logical generativeness of a subject—although this is an admittedly difficult statement from the point of view of epistemology. In commonsense terms, it amounts to the banality that grasp of a field of knowledge will never be better than the best that can be done with that field of knowledge. The effective power within a particular learner's grasp is what one seeks to discover by close analysis of how in fact he is going about his task of learning. Much of Piaget's research[3] seeks to discover just this property about children's learning and thinking. There is an interesting relation between economy and power. Theoretically, the two are independent: indeed, it is clear that a structure may be economical but powerless. But it is rare for a powerful structuring technique in any field to be uneconomical. This is what leads to the canon of parsimony and the faith shared by many scientists that nature is simple: perhaps it is only when nature can be made reasonably simple that it can be understood. The power of a representation can also be described as its capacity, in the hands of a learner, to connect matters that, on the surface, seem quite separate. This is especially crucial in mathematics, and we shall return to the matter later.

[2] Margaret Donaldson, *A Study of Children's Thinking* (London: Tavistock Publications, 1963).

[3] Jean Piaget, *The Child's Conception of Number* (New York: Humanities Press, 1952).

SEQUENCE AND ITS USES

Instruction consists of leading the learner through a sequence of statements and restatements of a problem or body of knowledge that increase the learner's ability to grasp, transform, and transfer what he is learning. In short, the sequence in which a learner encounters materials within a domain of knowledge affects the difficulty he will have in achieving mastery.

There are usually various sequences that are equivalent in their ease and difficulty for learners. There is no unique sequence for all learners, and the optimum in any particular case will depend upon a variety of factors, including past learning, stage of development, nature of the material, and individual differences.

If it is true that the usual course of intellectual development moves from enactive through iconic to symbolic representation of the world,[4] it is likely that an optimum sequence will progress in the same direction. Obviously, this is a conservative doctrine. For when the learner has a well-developed symbolic system, it may be possible to by-pass the first two stages. But one does so with the risk that the learner may not possess the imagery to fall back on when his symbolic transformations fail to achieve a goal in problem solving.

Exploration of alternatives will necessarily be affected by the sequence in which material to be learned becomes available to the learner. When the learner should be encouraged to explore alternatives widely and when he should be encouraged to concentrate on the implications of a single alternative hypothesis is an empirical question, to which we shall return.

Reverting to the earlier discussion of activation and the

---

[4] Jerome S. Bruner, "The Course of Cognitive Growth," *American Psychologist,* 19:1–15 (January 1964).

maintenance of interest, it is necessary to specify in any sequences the level of uncertainty and tension that must be present to initiate problem-solving behavior, and what conditions are required to keep active problem solving going. This again is an empirical question.

Optimal sequences, as already stated, cannot be specified independently of the criterion in terms of which final learning is to be judged. A classification of such criteria will include at least the following: speed of learning; resistance to forgetting; transferability of what has been learned to new instances; form of representation in terms of which what has been learned is to be expressed; economy of what has been learned in terms of cognitive strain imposed; effective power of what has been learned in terms of its generativeness of new hypotheses and combinations. Achieving one of these goals does not necessarily bring one closer to others; speed of learning, for example, is sometimes antithetical to transfer or to economy.

THE FORM AND PACING OF REINFORCEMENT

Learning depends upon knowledge of results at a time when and at a place where the knowledge can be used for correction. Instruction increases the appropriate timing and placing of corrective knowledge.

"Knowledge of results" is useful or not depending upon when and where the learner receives the corrective information, under what conditions such corrective information can be used, even assuming appropriateness of time and place of receipt, and the form in which the corrective information is received.

Learning and problem solving are divisible into phases. These have been described in various ways by different writers. But all the descriptions agree on one essential feature: that there is a cycle involving the formulation of a testing procedure or trial, the operation of this testing procedure, and the comparison of the results of the test with some criterion. It has variously been called trial-and-error, means-end testing, trial-and-check, discrepancy reduction, test-operate-test-exit (TOTE), hypothesis testing, and so on. These "units," moreover, can readily be characterized as hierarchically organized: we seek to cancel the unknowns in an equation in order to simplify the expression in order to solve the equation in order to get through the course in order to get our degree in order to get a decent job in order to lead the good life. Knowledge of results should come at that point in a problem-solving episode when the person is comparing the results of his try-out with some criterion of what he seeks to achieve. Knowledge of results given before this point either cannot be understood or must be carried as extra freight in immediate memory. Knowledge given after this point may be too late to guide the choice of a next hypothesis or trial. But knowledge of results must, to be useful, provide information not only on whether or not one's particular act produced success but also on whether the act is in fact leading one through the hierarchy of goals one is seeking to achieve. This is not to say that when we cancel the term in that equation we need to know whether it will all lead eventually to the good life. Yet there should at least be some "lead notice" available as to whether or not cancelation is on the right general track. It is here that the tutor has a special role. For most learning starts off rather piecemeal without the integration of component acts or elements. Usually the learner can tell whether a particular cycle of activity has worked— feedback from specific events is fairly simple—but often he cannot tell whether this completed cycle is leading to the eventual goal. It is interesting that one of the nonrigorous short cuts to problem solution, basic rules of "heuristic," stated in Polya's noted book[5] has to do with defining the overall problem. To sum up, then, instruction uniquely provides information to the

[5] Gyorgy Polya, *How To Solve It,* 2nd ed. (New York: Doubleday, 1957).

learner about the higher-order relevance of his efforts. In time, to be sure, the learner must develop techniques for obtaining such higher-order corrective information on his own, for instruction and its aids must eventually come to an end. And, finally, if the problem solver is to take over this function, it is necessary for him to learn to recognize when he does not comprehend and, as Roger Brown[6] has suggested, to signal incomprehension to the tutor so that he can be helped. In time, the signaling of incomprehension becomes a self-signaling and equivalent to a temporary stop order.

The ability of problem solvers to use information correctively is known to vary as a function of their internal state. One state in which information is least useful is that of strong drive and anxiety. There is a sufficient body of research to establish this point beyond reasonable doubt.[7] Another such state has been referred to as "functional fixedness"—a problem solver is, in effect, using corrective information exclusively for the evaluation of one single hypothesis that happens to be wrong. The usual example is treating an object in terms of its conventional significance when it must be treated in a new context—we fail to use a hammer as a bob for a pendulum because it is "fixed" in our thinking as a hammer. Numerous studies point to the fact that during such a period there is a remarkable intractability or even incorrigibility to problem solving. There is some evidence to indicate that high drive and anxiety lead one to be more prone to functional fixedness. It is obvious that corrective information of the usual type, straight feedback, is least useful during such states, and that an adequate instructional strategy aims at terminating the interfering state by special means before continuing with the usual pro-

6 Roger Brown, *Social Psychology* (New York: Free Press of Glencoe, 1965), chapter 7, "From Codability to Coding Ability."

7 For full documentation, see Jerome S. Bruner, "Some Theorems on Instruction Illustrated with Reference to Mathematics," *Sixty-third Yearbook of the National Society for the Study of Education,* Part I (Chicago: University of Chicago Press, 1964), pp. 306–335.

vision of correction. In such cases, instruction verges on a kind of therapy, and it is perhaps because of this therapeutic need that one often finds therapylike advice in lists of aids for problem solvers, like the suggestion of George Humphrey[8] that one turn away from the problem when it is proving too difficult.

If information is to be used effectively, it must be translated into the learner's way of attempting to solve a problem. If such translatability is not present, then the information is simply useless. Telling a neophyte skier to "shift to his uphill edges" when he cannot distinguish which edges he is traveling on provides no help, whereas simply telling him to lean into the hill may succeed. Or, in the cognitive sphere, there is by now an impressive body of evidence that indicates that "negative information"—information about what something is *not*—is peculiarly unhelpful to a person seeking to master a concept. Though it is logically usable, it is psychologically useless. Translatability of corrective information can in principle also be applied to the form of representation and its economy. If learning or problem solving is proceeding in one mode—enactive, iconic or symbolic—corrective information must be provided either in the same mode or in one that translates into it. Corrective information that exceeds the information-processing capacities of a learner is obviously wasteful.

Finally, it is necessary to reiterate one general point already made in passing. Instruction is a provisional state that has as its object to make the learner or problem solver self-sufficient. Any regimen of correction carries the danger that the learner may become permanently dependent upon the tutor's correction. The tutor must correct the learner in a fashion that eventually makes it possible for the learner to take over the corrective function himself. Otherwise the result of instruction is to create a form of mastery that is contingent upon the perpetual presence of a teacher.

[8] George Humphrey, *Directed Thinking* (New York: Dodd, Mead, 1948).

SELECTED ILLUSTRATIONS FROM MATHEMATICS

Before turning to the task of illustrating some of the points raised, a word is in order about what is intended by such illustration. During the last decade much work has gone into the mathematics curriculum. One need only mention the curriculum projects that are better known to appreciate the magnitude of the effort—the School Mathematics Study Group, the University of Illinois Committee on School Mathematics, the several projects of Educational Services Incorporated, the Madison Project, the African Mathematics Project, the University of Maryland Mathematics Project, the University of Illinois Arithmetic Project, and the Stanford Project. From this activity, it would be possible to choose illustrations for many purposes. Illustration in such a context in no sense constitutes evidence.

For the fact of the matter is that the evidence available on factors affecting the learning of mathematics is still very sparse. Research on the instructional process—in mathematics as in all disciplines—has not been carried out in connection with the building of curricula. As noted, psychologists have come upon the scene, armed with evaluative devices, only after a curriculum has already been put into operation. Surely it would be more efficient and more useful if embryonic instructional materials could be tried out under experimental conditions so that revision and correction could be based upon immediate knowledge of results.

By means of systematic observational studies—work close in spirit to that of Piaget and of ethologists like Tinbergen[9]— investigators could obtain information sufficiently detailed to allow them to discern how the student grasps what has been presented, what his systematic errors are, and how these are overcome. Insofar as one is able to formalize, in terms of a

[9] Nikolaas Tinbergen, *Social Behavior in Animals* (New York: John Wiley & Sons, 1953).

theory of learning or concept attainment, the nature of the systematic errors and the strategies of correction employed, one is thereby enabled to vary systematically the conditions that may be affecting learning and to build these factors directly into one's curriculum practice. Nor need such studies remain purely observational. Often it is possible to build one's mathematics materials into a programmed form and obtain a detailed behavioral record for analysis.

To make clear what is intended by a detailed analysis of the process of learning, an example from the work of Patrick Suppes[10] will be helpful. He has observed, for example, that the form $3 + x = 8$ is easier for children to deal with than the form $x + 3 = 8$, and while the finding may on the surface seem trivial, closer inspection shows that it is not. Does the difficulty come in dealing with an unknown at the beginning of an expression or from the transfer of linguistic habits from ordinary English, where sentences are easier to complete when a term is deleted from the middle than from beginning of the sentence? The issue of where uncertainty can best be tolerated and the issue of the possible interference between linguistic habits and mathematical habits are certainly worthy of careful and detailed study.

Let me turn now to some illustrations from mathematics that have the effect of pointing up problems raised in the theorems and hypotheses earlier presented. They are not evidence of anything, only ways of locating what might be worth closer study.[11]

[10] Patrick Suppes, "Towards a Behavioral Psychology of Mathematics Thinking," in J. Bruner, ed., *Learning about Learning,* U.S. Office of Education monograph, in press.

[11] For a closer discussion of some of the observations mentioned in what follows, the reader is referred to Bruner, "The Course of Cognitive Growth," and to Jerome S. Bruner and Helen Kenney, "Representation and Mathematics Learning," in L. Morrisett and J. Vinsonhaler, eds., *Mathematical Learning,* Monographs of the Society for Research in Child Development, 30 (University of Chicago Press, 1965), pp. 50–59. The general "bias" on which

Rather than presenting observations drawn from different contexts, I shall confine the discussion to one particular study carried out on a small group of children.[12] The observations to be reported were made on four eight-year-old children, two boys and two girls, who were given an hour of daily instruction in mathematics four times a week for six weeks. The children were in the IQ range of 120–130, and they were all enrolled in the third grade of a private school that emphasized instruction designed to foster independent problem solving. They were all from middle-class professional homes. The "teacher" of the class was a well-known research mathematician (Z. P. Dienes), his assistant a professor of psychology at Harvard who has worked long and hard on human thought processes.

Each child worked at a corner table in a generous-sized room. Next to each child sat a tutor-observer, trained in psychology and with sufficient background in college mathematics to understand the underlying mathematics being taught. In the middle of the room was a large table with a supply of blocks and balance beams and cups and beans and chalk that served as instructional aids. In the course of the six weeks, the children were given instruction in factoring, in the distributive and commutative properties of addition and multiplication, and finally in quadratic functions.

Each child had available a series of graded problem cards which he could go through at his own pace. The cards gave directions for different kinds of exercises, using the materials mentioned above. The instructor and his assistant circulated

---

these observations are based is contained in Jerome S. Bruner, *The Process of Education* (Cambridge: Harvard University Press, 1960), and in J. S. Bruner, J. J. Goodnow, and G. A. Austin, *A Study of Thinking* (New York: John Wiley & Sons, 1956).

[12] I am grateful to Z. P. Dienes, Samuel Anderson, Eleanor Duckworth, and Joan Rigney Hornsby for their help in designing and carrying out this study. Dr. Dienes particularly formed our thinking about the mode of presenting the mathematical materials.

from table to table helping as needed, and each tutor-observer similarly assisted as needed. The problem sequences were designed to provide, first, an appreciation of mathematical ideas through concrete constructions involving materials of various kinds. From such constructions, the child was encouraged to form perceptual images of the mathematical idea in terms of the forms that had been constructed. The child was then further encouraged to develop or adopt a notation for describing his construction. After such a cycle, a child moved on to the construction of a further embodiment of the idea on which he was working, one that was mathematically isomorphic with what he had learned, though expressed in different materials and with altered appearance. When such a new topic was introduced, the children were given a chance to discover its connection with what had gone before and shown how to extend the notational system used before. Careful minute-by-minute records were kept of the proceedings, along with photographs of the children's constructions.

In no sense can the children, the teachers, the classroom, or the mathematics be said to be typical of what occurs in third grade. Four children rarely have six teachers, nor do eight-year-olds ordinarily get into quadratic functions. But our concern is with the processes involved in mathematical learning, and not with typicality. It seems quite reasonable to suppose that the thought processes that were going on in the children are quite ordinary among eight-year-old human beings.

ACTIVATING PROBLEM SOLVING

One of the first tasks faced in this study was to gain and hold the child's interest and to lead him to problem-solving activity. At the same time, there was a specific objective to be achieved —to teach the children factoring in such a way that they would have this component skill in an accessible form to use in the solution of problems. It is impossible to say on the basis of our experience whether the method we employed was the best one, but in any case it appeared to work.

A considerable part of the job of activation had already been done before ever we saw the children. They had working models of exploratory adults in their teachers and their parents. They had no particular resistance to trying out and rejecting hypotheses. The principal problem we faced as teachers who outnumbered the students was to keep the children from converting the task into one where they would become dependent upon us. All of us had had the experience of working with children from less intellectually stimulating backgrounds where there had been less emphasis upon intellectual autonomy, and the contrast was appreciable. Indeed, I can only repeat that where predisposition to learning was concerned, the children in the study were almost specifically trained for the kind of approach we were about to use—an approach with strong emphasis on independence, on self-pacing, on reflectiveness. Had we used a more authoritarian, more mnemonic approach with our group, we would have had to prepare the ground. As it was, the task had already been well begun.

The first learning task introduced was one having to do with the different ways in which a set of cubic blocks could be arranged as "flats" (laid out in rectangular forms on the table, not more than one cube high) and in "walls" and "buildings." The problem has an interesting uncertainty to it, and the children were challenged to determine whether they had exhausted all the possible ways of laying things out. Unquestionably they picked up some zest from the evident curiosity of their teachers as well. After a certain amount of time, the children were encouraged to start keeping a written record of the different shapes they could make, and what their dimensions were. Certain numbers of cubes proved intractable to re-forming (the primes, of course), and others proved combinable in interesting ways—three rows of three cubes made nine, three layers of these nine "flats" had the dimensions of $3 \times 3 \times 3$, and so on. The idea of factoring was soon grasped, and with very little guidance the children went on to interesting conjectures about distributiveness. The task had its own direction built into it in the sense that it had a clear terminus: how arrange a set of cubes in regular two- or three-dimensional forms? It also had the added feature that the idea of alternatives was built in: what are the different ways of achieving such regularity? As the children gained in skill, they shifted to other ways of laying out cubes—in pyramids, in triangles where the cubes were treated as "diamonds," and so on. At this stage of the game, it was necessary to judge in each case whether the child should be let alone to discover on his own.

We shall see, when we come to discuss the balance beam, that the idea of factoring was further deepened by being applied to a "new" problem. I mention the point here because it relates to the importance of *maintaining* a problem-solving set that runs in a continuous direction. It is often the case that novelty must be introduced in order that the enterprise be continued. In the case of the balance beam, the task was to discover the different combinations of rings that could be put on one side of the balance beam to balance a single ring placed on hook 9. In effect, this is the same problem as asking the different ways in which nine blocks can be arranged. But it is in a different guise, and the new embodiment seems capable of stimulating interest even though it is isomorphic with something else that has been explored to the border of satiety.

STRUCTURE AND SEQUENCE

We can best illustrate the points made at the outset by reference to our teaching of quadratic equations to the four children we studied. Each child was provided with building

materials. These were large flat squares made of wood whose
dimensions were unspecified and described simply as "unknown, or *x* long and *x* wide." There were also a large number
of strips of wood that were as long as the sides of the square
and were described arbitrarily as having a width of "1" or
simply as "1 by *x*." And there was a supply of little squares
with sides equal to the width "1" of the strips, thus "1 by 1."
The reader should be warned that the presentation of these
materials is not as simple as all that. To begin with, it is
necessary to convince the children that we really do not know
and do not *care* what the metric size of the big square is, that
rulers are of no interest. A certain humor helps establish in
the pupils a proper contempt for measuring in this context, and
the snob appeal of simply calling an unknown by the name
"*x*" is very great. From there on, the children readily discover
for themselves that the long strips are *x* long—by correspondence. They take on faith (as they should) that the narrow
dimension is "1," but that they grasp its arbitrariness is clear
from one child's declaration of the number of such "1" widths
that made an *x*. As for "1 by 1" little squares, that too is established by simple correspondence with the narrow dimension of
the "1 by *x*" strips. It is horseback method, but quite good
mathematics.

The child is asked whether he can make a square bigger than

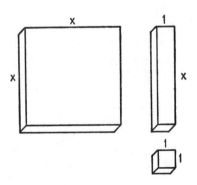

the x by x square, using the materials at hand. He very quickly
builds squares with designs like those illustrated below. We ask
him to record how much wood is needed for each larger square
and how long and wide each square is.

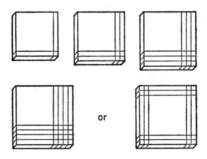

or

He describes one of his constructed squares: very concretely
the pieces are counted out: "an x-square, two x-strips, and a
one square," or "an x-square, four x-strips, and four ones," or
"an x-square, six x-strips and nine ones," and so forth. We
help him with language and show him a way to write it down.
The big square is an "$x\square$," the long strips are "$1x$" or simply
"x," and the little squares are "one squares" or "one by one"
or, better still, simply "1." And the expression "and" can be
shortened to $+$. And so he can write out the recipe for a constructed square as $x\square + 4x + 4$. At this stage, these are merely
names put together in little sentences. How wide and long is
the square in question? This the child can readily measure off
—an x and 2, or $x + 2$, and so the whole thing is $(x + 2)\square$.
Brackets are not so easily grasped. But soon the child is able to
put down his first equality: $(x + 2)\square = x\square + 4x + 4$. Virtually everything has a referent that can be pointed to with a
finger. He has a notational system into which he can translate
the image he has constructed.

Now we go on to making bigger squares, and each square
the child makes he is to describe in terms of what wood went
into it and how wide and how long it is. It takes some ruled

sheets to get the child to keep his record so that he can go back and inspect it for what it may reveal, and he is encouraged to go back and look at the record and at the constructions they stand for.

Imagine now a list such as the following, again a product of the child's own constructing:

$$x^\square + 2x + 1 \text{ is } x + 1 \text{ by } x + 1$$
$$x^\square + 4x + 4 \text{ is } x + 2 \text{ by } x + 2$$
$$x^\square + 6x + 9 \text{ is } x + 3 \text{ by } x + 3$$
$$x^\square + 8x + 16 \text{ is } x + 4 \text{ by } x + 4$$

It is almost impossible for him not to make some discoveries about the numbers: that the x values go up 2, 4, 6, 8, and the units values go up 1, 4, 9, 16, and the dimensions increase by additions to x of 1, 2, 3, 4. The syntactical insights about regularity in notation are matched by perceptual-manipulative insights about the material referents.

After a while, some new manipulations occur that provide the child with a further basis for notational progress. He takes the square $(x + 2)^2$ and reconstructs it in a new way. One may ask whether this is constructive manipulation, and whether it is proper factoring. But the child is learning that the same amount of wood can build quite strikingly different patterns and remain the same amount of wood—even though it also has a different notational expression. Where does the language begin and the manipulation of materials stop? The interplay is continuous. We shall return to this same example later.

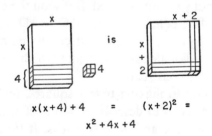

$$x(x+4) + 4 \quad = \quad (x+2)^2 =$$
$$x^2 + 4x + 4$$

What is now a problem is how to "detach" the notation that the child has learned from the concrete, visible, manipulable embodiment to which it refers—the wood. For if the child is to deal with mathematical properties he will have to deal with symbols per se, else he will be limited to the narrow and rather trivial range of symbolism that can be given direct (and only partial) visual embodiment. Concepts such as x^2 and x^3 may be given a visualizable referent, but what of x^n ?

How do children wean themselves from the perceptual embodiment to the symbolic notation? Perhaps it is partly explained in the nature of variation and contrast.

The child is shown the balance beam again and told: "Choose any hook on one side and put the same number of rings on it as the number the hook is away from the middle. Now balance it with rings placed on the other side. Keep a record." Recall that the balance beam is familiar from work on factoring and that the child knows that 2 rings on 9 balances 9 on 2 or m rings on n balances n on m. He is back to construction. Can anything be constructed on the balance beam that is like the squares? With little effort, the following translation is made. Suppose x is 5. Then 5 rings on hook 5 is x^2, 5 rings on hook 4 is $4x$, and 4 rings on hook 1 is 4: $x^2 + 4x + 4$. How can we find whether this is like a square that is $x + 2$ wide by $x + 2$ long, as before? Well, if x is 5, then $x + 2$ is 7, and so 7 rings on hook 7. And nature obliges —the beam balances. One notation works for two strikingly

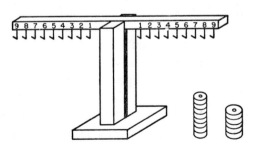

different constructions and perceptual events. Notation, with its broader equivalency, is clearly more economical than reference to embodiments. There is little resistance to using this more convenient language. And now construction can begin—commutative and distributive properties of equations can be explored: $x(x + 4) + 4 = x^2 + 4x + 4$, so that $x + 4$ rings on hook x plus 4 rings on hook 1 will also balance. The child if he wishes can also go back to the wood and find that the same materials can make the designs illustrated earlier.

Contrast is the vehicle by which the obvious that is too obvious to be appreciated can be made noticeable again. A discovery by an eight-year-old girl illustrates the matter. "Yes, 4×6 equals 6×4 in numbers, like in one way six eskimos in each of four igloos is the same as four in each of six igloos. But a venetian blind *isn't* the same as a blind Venetian." By recognizing the noncommutative property of much of our ordinary language, the commutative property of a mathematical language can be partly grasped. But it is still only a partial insight into commutativity and noncommutativity. Had we wished to develop the distinction more deeply we might have proceeded concretely to a contrast between sets of operations that can be carried out in any sequence—like the order in which letters are put in a post box or in which we see different movies—and operations that have a noncommutative order—like putting on shoes and socks—where one must precede the other. The child could be taken from there to a more general idea of commutative and noncommutative cases and to ways of dealing with a notation for them, perhaps by identical sets and ordered identical sets.

We need not reiterate what must be obvious from this sequence. The object was to begin with an enactive representation of quadratics—something that could literally be "done" or built—and to move from there to an iconic representation, however restricted. Along the way, notation was developed and, by the use of variation and contrast, converted into a properly symbolic system. Again, the object was to start with as economical a representation as possible and to increase complexity only when there was some way for the child to relate the complex instance to something simpler that had gone before.

What was so striking in the performance of the children was their initial inability to represent things to themselves in a way that transcended immediate perceptual grasp. The achievement of more comprehensive insight requires, we think, the building of a mediating representational structure that transcends such immediate imagery, that renders a sequence of acts and images unitary and simultaneous. The children always began by constructing an embodiment of some concept, building a concrete model for purposes of operational definition. The fruit of the construction was an image and some operations that "stood for" the concept. From there on, the task was to provide means of representation that were free of particular manipulations and specific images. Only symbolic operations provide the means of representing an idea in this way. But consider this matter for a moment.

We have already remarked that by giving the child multiple embodiments of the same general idea expressed in a common notation we lead him to "empty" the concept of specific sensory properties until he is able to grasp its abstract properties. But surely this is not the best way of describing the child's increasing development of insight. The growth of such abstractions is important. But what struck us about the children as we observed them is that they not only understood the abstractions they had learned but also had a store of concrete images that served to exemplify the abstractions. When they searched for a way to deal with new problems, the task was usually carried out not simply by abstract means but also by "matching up" images. An example will help here. In going from the wood-blocks embodiment of the quadratic to the balance-beam embodiment, it was interesting that the children would "equate" concrete features of one with concrete features of another. One side of the balance beam "stood for" the amount of wood, the other side for the sides of the square. These were important concrete props on which they leaned. We have been told by research mathematicians that the same use of props— heuristics—holds for them, that they have preferred ways of imaging certain problems while other problems are handled silently or in terms of an imagery of the symbolism on a page.

We reached the tentative conclusion that it was probably necessary for a child, learning mathematics, to have not only a firm sense of the abstraction underlying what he was working on, but also a good stock of visual images for embodying them. For without the latter it is difficult to track correspondences and to check what one is doing symbolically. We had occasion, again with the help of Dr. Dienes, to teach a group of ten nine-year-olds the elements of group theory. To embody the idea of a mathematical group initially, we gave them the example of a four-group made up of the following four maneuvers. A book was the vehicle, a book with an arrow up the middle of its front cover. The four maneuvers were rotating the book a quarter turn to the left, rotating it a quarter turn to the right, rotating it a half turn (without regard to direction of rotation), and letting it stay in the position it was in. They were quick to grasp the important property of such a mathematical group: that any sequence of maneuvers made could be reproduced from the starting position by a single move. This is not the usual way in which this property is described mathematically, but it served well for the children. We contrasted this elegant property with a series of our moves that did *not* constitute a mathematical group—indeed, they provided the counter example themselves by proposing a one-third turn left, one-third turn right, half turn either way, and stay. It was soon apparent that it did not work. We set the children the task of making games of four maneuvers, six maneuvers, and so on, that had the property of a "closed" game, as we call it—one in which the result of any combination of moves can be achieved by a single move. They were, of course, highly ingenious. But what soon became apparent was that they needed some aid in imagery—in this case an imagery notation—that would allow them to keep track and then to discover whether some new game was an isomorph of one they had already developed. The prop in this case was, of course, the matrix, listing the moves possible across the top and then listing them down the side, thus making it easily possible to check whether each combination of pairs of moves could be reproduced by a single move. The matrix in this case is a crutch or heuristic and as such has nothing to do with the abstraction of the mathematical group, yet it was enormously useful to them not only for keeping track but also for comparing one group with another for correspondence. The matrix with which they started looked like this:

	s	a	b	c	
	s	a	b	c	s = stay
s	s	a	b	c	a = quarter-turn left
a	a	c	s	b	b = quarter-turn right
b	b	s	c	a	c = half-turn
c	c	b	a	s	

Are there any four-groups with a different structure? It is extremely difficult to deal with such a question without the aid of this housekeeping matrix as a vehicle for spotting correspondence. What about a game in which a cube can be left where it is, rotated 180° on its vertical axis, rotated 180° on its horizontal axis, and rotated 180° on each of its four cubic diagonals? Is it a group? Can it be simplified to a smaller number of maneuvers? Does it contain the group described above?

In sum, then, while the development of insight into mathematics in our group of children depended upon their development of "example-free" abstractions, this did not lead them to give up their imagery. Quite to the contrary, we had the impression that their enriched imagery was very useful to them in dealing with new problems.

We would suggest that learning mathematics reflects a good deal about intellectual development. It begins with instrumental activity, a kind of definition of things by doing them. Such operations become represented and summarized in the form of particular images. Finally, and with the help of a symbolic notation that remains invariant across transformations in imagery, the learner comes to grasp the formal or abstract properties of the things he is dealing with. But while, once abstraction is achieved, the learner becomes free in a certain measure of the surface appearance of things, he nonetheless continues to rely upon the stock of imagery he has built en route to abstract mastery. It is this stock of imagery that permits him to work at the level of heuristic, through convenient and nonrigorous means of exploring problems and relating them to problems already mastered.

REINFORCEMENT AND FEEDBACK

With respect to corrective information, there is something particularly happy about the exercises we chose to use. In learning quadratics by the use of our blocks and then by the aid of the balance beam, children were enabled by immediate test to determine whether they had "got there." A collection of square pieces of wood is aggregated in a form that either makes a square or doesn't, and the child can see it immediately. So too with a balance beam: it either balances or it does not. There is no instructor intervening between the learner and the materials.

But note well that the instructor had to enter in several ways. In the first place, he determined within quite constrained limits the nature of the sequences, so that the children would have the greatest chance of seeing the relation of what went before to what was up now. Whether we succeeded well in these sequences we do not know—save that the children learned some elegant mathematics in a fairly short time. What guided us was some sort of psychological-mathematical intuition, and while that may be satisfactory for such engineering as we did, it is certainly not satisfactory from the point of view of understanding how to do it better.

We failed on several occasions, as judged by the lagging interest of a particular child, when we wanted to be sure that the child had really understood something. Our most glaring failure was in trying to get across in symbolic form (probably too early) the idea of distributiveness—that $a + (b + c)$ and $(a + b) + c$ could be treated as equivalent. One of our cleverest young pupils commented at the beginning of an hour, with a groan, "Oh, they're distributing the distributive law again." In fact, our difficulty came from a misjudgment of the importance of giving them a symbolic mode for correcting iconic constructions. We were too eager to be sure that they sensed the notational analogue of the factoring constructions they had been making and which they understood at the iconic level so well that further construction was proving a bore.

We have few fresh observations to report on the matter of overdrive and anxiety. One of our pupils had a rather strong push about mathematics from his father at home. He was the child who, on the first day, had to demonstrate his prowess by multiplying two large and ugly numbers on the board, announcing the while, "I know a lot of math." He was probably our best student, but he made no progress until he got over the idea that what was needed was hard computation. It was he, too, who complained that the blocks used for quadratics *had* to have *some* size. But once he was willing to play with unknowns as "x" he showed considerable power. His father was our unwitting ally at this point, for he told him that "x's" were from algebra, which was a subject most children took in high school.

Perhaps the greatest problem one has in an experiment of this sort is to keep out of the way, to prevent oneself from becoming a perennial source of information, interfering with the child's ability to take over the role of being his own corrector. But each classroom situation is unique in this way, and each dyad of teacher and pupil. Some of the teacher-pupil pairs became quite charged with dependency; in others the child or the teacher resisted. But that is another story.

SOME CONCLUSIONS

A first and obvious conclusion is that one must take into account the issues of predisposition, structure, sequence, and reinforcement in preparing curriculum materials—whether one is concerned with writing a textbook, a lesson plan, a unit of instruction, a program, or, indeed, a conversation with didactic ends in view. But this obvious conclusion suggests some rather nonobvious implications.

The type of supporting research that permits one to assess how well one is succeeding in the management of relevant instructional variables requires a constant and close collaboration of teacher, subject-matter specialist, and psychologist. As intimated earlier, a curriculum should be prepared jointly by the subject-matter expert, the teacher, and the psychologist, with due regard for the inherent structure of the material, its sequencing, the psychological pacing of reinforcement, and the building and maintaining of predispositions to problem solving. As the curriculum is being built, it must be tested in detail by close observational and experimental methods to assess not simply whether children are "achieving" but rather what they are making of the material and how they are organizing it. It is on the basis of "testing as you go" that revision is made. It is this procedure that puts the evaluation process at a time when and place where its results can be used for correction while the curriculum is being constructed.

Only passing reference has been made to the issue of individual differences. Quite plainly, they exist in massive degree —in the extent to which children have problem-solving predispositions, in the degree of their interest, in the skills that they bring to any concrete task, in their preferred mode of representing things, in their ability to move easily through any particular sequence, and in the degree to which they are initially dependent upon extrinsic reinforcement from the teacher. The fact of individual differences argues for pluralism and for an enlightened opportunism in the materials and methods of instruction. Earlier we asserted, rather off-handedly, that no single ideal sequence exists for any group of children. The conclusion to be drawn from that assertion is not that it is impossible to put together a curriculum that would satisfy a group of children or a cross-section of children. Rather, it is that if a curriculum is to be effective in the classroom it must contain different ways of activating children, different ways of presenting sequences, different opportunities for some children to "skip" parts while others work their way through, different ways of putting things. A curriculum, in short, must contain many tracks leading to the same general goal.

Our illustrations have been taken from mathematics, but there are some generalizations that go beyond to other fields. The first is that it took the efforts of many highly talented mathematicians to discern the underlying structure of the mathematics that was to be taught. That is to say, the simplicity of a mathematics curriculum rests upon the history and development of mathematics itself. But even so glorious an intellectual tradition as that of mathematics was not enough. For while many virtues have been discovered for numbers to the base 10, students cannot appreciate such virtues until they recognize that the base 10 was not handed down from the mountain by some mathematical God. It is when the student learns to work in different number bases that the base 10 is recognized for the achievement that it is.

Finally, a theory of instruction seeks to take account of the fact that a curriculum reflects not only the nature of knowledge itself but also the nature of the knower and of the knowledge-getting process. It is the enterprise par excellence where the line between subject matter and method grows necessarily indistinct. A body of knowledge, enshrined in a university faculty and embodied in a series of authoritative volumes, is the result of much prior intellectual activity. To instruct someone in these disciplines is not a matter of getting him to commit results to mind. Rather, it is to teach him to participate in the process that makes possible the establishment of knowledge. We teach a subject not to produce little living libraries on that subject, but rather to get a student to think mathematically for himself, to consider matters as an historian does, to take part in the process of knowledge-getting. Knowing is a process, not a product.

Chapter 4

Man:
A Course of Study

THERE IS a dilemma in describing a course of study. One must begin by setting forth the intellectual substance of what is to be taught, else there can be no sense of what challenges and shapes the curiosity of the student. Yet the moment one succumbs to the temptation to "get across" the subject, at that moment the ingredient of pedagogy is in jeopardy. For it is only in a trivial sense that one gives a course to "get something across," merely to impart information. There are better means to that end than teaching. Unless the learner also masters himself, disciplines his taste, deepens his view of the world, the "something" that is got across is hardly worth the effort of transmission.

The more elementary a course and the younger its students, the more serious must be its pedagogical aim of forming the intellectual powers of those whom it serves. It is as important that a good mathematics course be justified by the intellectual discipline it provides or the honesty it promotes as by the mathematics it transmits. Indeed, neither can be accomplished without the other.

With these things in mind, let me describe the substance or structure of a course in social studies now in the process of construction, parts of which have been taught to children in grade five. What is presented here is a blueprint. It may turn out to be the case, as modifications are made during tryout and testing, that the final course will have a quite different shape. It is plain, in the very form of its construction, that the course will have different form when taught by different teachers. Indeed, it is constructed in modules so that a teacher *can* (indeed, is encouraged to) place her own signature upon it. I do not hesitate to present what I know to be an unfinished course, for it is the process of curriculum making that is of concern here, and not the product. The present effort, carried out under the aegis of Educational Services Incorporated with grants from the Ford Foundation and the National Science Foundation, is very much in process—as we shall see in the final essay.

STRUCTURE OF THE COURSE

The content of the course is man: his nature as a species, the forces that shaped and continue to shape his humanity. Three questions recur throughout:

What is human about human beings?

How did they get that way?

How can they be made more so?

We seek exercises and materials through which our pupils can learn wherein man is distinctive in his adaptation to the world, and wherein there is discernible continuity between him and his animal forebears. For man represents that crucial point in evolution where adaptation is achieved by the vehicle of culture, and only in a minor way by further changes in his morphology. Yet there are chemical tides that run in his blood that are as ancient as the reptiles. We make every effort at the outset to *tell* the children where we hope to travel with them. Yet little of such recounting gets through. Much more useful, we have found, is to pose the three questions directly to the children so that their own views can be brought into the open and so that they can establish some points of view of their own.

In pursuit of our questions we proceed to explore five subjects, each closely associated with the evolution of man as a species, each defining at once the distinctiveness of man and his potentiality for further evolution. The five great humanizing forces are tool making, language, social organization, the management of man's prolonged childhood, and man's urge to explain his world. It has been our first lesson in teaching that no pupil, however eager, can appreciate the relevance of, say, tool making in human evolution without first grasping the fundamental concept of a tool—or what a language is, or a myth, or social organization. These are not obvious matters. So we are involved not only in teaching the role of tools or language in the emergence of man, but, as a necessary precondition for doing so, in setting forth the fundamentals of linguistics or the theory of tools. And it is as often as not the case that (as with the "theory of tools") we must solve a formidable intellectual problem ourselves in order to be able to help our pupils do the same.

While one readily singles out these five massive contributors to man's humanization, under no circumstances can they be put into airtight compartments. Human kinship is distinctively different from what we find in a primate troop, and is based on a system of classification that is inconceivable without language. Distinctions between those who are permitted or favored as mates and those who are ruled out as "incestuous" are governed by a system of naming that can only be mastered by one who can handle a human language—as in the famous case of mother's brother's daughter being the favored bride in many patrilineal societies. Or, to take another connection, tool use enhances the division of labor in a society, and division of labor in turn affects kinship. Indeed, language itself is only clearly appreciated by reference to its acquisition in the uniquely human interaction between child and parent. And obviously the nature of man's world view, whether formulated in myth or in science, depends upon and is constrained by the nature of human language. So while each domain can be treated as a separate set of ideas, as we shall see, success in teaching depends upon making it possible for children to have a sense of their interaction.

The choice of topic is partly fortuitous—in the sense that it reflected the interests and knowledge of those of us who were involved. But beyond that, its emphasis on the "newer" behavioral sciences recognizes what in an earlier essay was described as the need for general principles in understanding man and society lest we be overwhelmed by the richness of historical record.

LANGUAGE

Teaching a decent beginning of modern linguistics to ten-year-olds is not easy, given the limit on time, but not as difficult as we had feared. There are certain pedagogic precautions to be respected if children are to be attracted by the subject. The subject must not, to begin with, be presented as a normative one—as an exercise in how things *should* be written or said. It must, moreover, be dissociated from such traditional grammar as the child has encountered. There is nothing so deadening as to have a child handle the form classes as traditional "parts of speech," "recognizing" one category of words as "nouns" and parroting, upon being asked what he means by a noun, that it is a "person, place, or thing." It is not that he is either right or wrong, but rather that he is as remote from the issue as somebody would be who attempted to account for grief over the assassination of a President by citing the Constitution on the division of powers. And finally, the discussion needs to remain close to the nature of language in use, its likely origin, and the functions it serves.

Whether it is true or not that a ten-year-old has a complete grammatical repertory, he is certainly capable of and delighted in intuitively recognizing linguistic phenomena when confronted with instances of them. The chief aid to such recognition is contrast—the opportunity to observe the oppositional features that are so much a characteristic of human language. What comes hard is to formulate these features conceptually, to go beyond the intuitive grasp of the native speaker to the more self-conscious understanding of the linguist. It is this task—getting children to look at and ponder the things they can notice in their language, long enough to understand them —that is most difficult, and it should not be pushed to the point of tedium.

Our section on language includes a consideration of what communication is—by contrasting how humans and animals manage to send and receive messages. The early sessions have proved lively, and in the course of them nearly every major issue of linguistics is raised and allowed to go begging. This preliminary exercise has the great virtue that it can be repeated on later occasions, when students have achieved varying levels of sophistication, with the result that they readily recognize how much progress they have made.

The opening session (or sessions, for students often want to continue the arguments over animals and humans) usually indicates which among several openings can best be pursued in later units. The discussion tends to lead naturally to the properties of communication systems in general, including human language. We have found that progress comes faster when the children have something with which to compare human language, and Von Frisch's description of the round dance and tail-wagging dance of the bee serves us well. In our preliminary work, we find that children come very swiftly to a discussion (in lay and intuitive terms) of such matters as how one refers by signs and symbols to "things," the difficulties of reference when what is referred to is not present to point to, the relative advantages of a voice-ear system, the difference between an inherited and a culturally transmitted language, and so on down the list of classic issues.

Our next objective is to present the powerful ideas of arbitrariness, of productivity, and of duality of patterning so called, the last the exclusive property of human language. We have approached arbitrariness by the conventional route of comparing how pictures, diagrams, charades, and words refer to things. There are nice jokes to be used, as in seeking to find some relation between length of name and size of child. With respect to productivity, we have had considerable initial success with two exercises. The first is with a lexicon containing four word classes (how, what, when, and where words), with a limited number of tokens of each type (by hand, by weapon, by trap, are tokens of the "how" type), and we use word-class orders to refer to different food-related activities. By this means we readily establish the notion of word *type* and *order* as two basic ideas. Children readily grasp the possibility of substituting tokens within a type. (Indeed, given the interest in secret codes based on substitution of words or letters for code breaking, they need little instruction on this score.)

Once the ideas of type and order are established, we begin the following amusing exercise to illustrate the interchangeability of language frames. We present:

1	2	3	4	5
The	man	ate	his	lunch
A	lady	wore	my	hat
This	doctor	broke	a	bottle
My	son	drove	our	car

and the children are now asked to provide "matching" examples. They can do so readily. They soon discover that so long as they pick words in the order 1 2 3 4 5, from any place in each column, something "sensible" can be got: even if it is silly or not true, like "My doctor wore a car" or "A lady ate a bottle," it is at least not "crazy," like "Man the lunch his ate."

Our students need no urging to construct new frames and to insert additional types into frames already set up (like a new first column the tokens of which include *did, can, has, will*). Interesting discoveries are made—such as the relative openness of some positions and the closed nature of others, and the difficulties of some tokens within a type. We hope to devise methods to help the children discover some of the deeper features of grammar, better to grasp what a language is—for example, that one can start with relatively simple sentence frames, "kernel sentences," and transform them successively into negatives, queries, and passives, or any two or even three of these, and that more complex forms can be returned to simpler forms by applying the transformations in reverse. Finally, a game has been devised (a game involving signaling at sea) to illustrate duality of patterning, that most difficult feature of human language. Each human language combines intrinsically meaningless sounds into a unique system of phonemes that make up words or morphemes. A change in a phoneme alters the meaning of a word. In English *rob* and *lob* are different words, but they would be the same word in Japanese, where *r* and *l* belong to the same phoneme, just as the plosive *p* of *pin* and the nonplosive *p* of *spin* are "the same" for us but not for others. In our game we set out to construct a language initially with a very limited set of phonemes as our building blocks. Three kinds of blocks can be arranged in various ways in a three-block frame, making twenty-seven possible "words" or morphemes. Some combinations mean things, some not. It is very quickly apparent to the children that the blocks as such "mean" nothing, but the frames do—or some do and some do not. We go from here to more complex notions of morphophonemics if the children are interested.

Later we move on to the question of how language is acquired by young humans. We use the considerable resources provided by recent studies of language acquisition to show the manner in which syntax emerges from certain very elementary forms. We hope to contrast human language learning with the learning of baboons mastering their signaling system. The subtle problems of "traditional" and "hereditary" transmission are bound to emerge.

Finally, and with the benefit of the children's increased insight into the nature of language, we return to the question of the origins and functions of human language and the role of language in shaping human characteristics and thought. We hope first to cover the newly available materials on the universal characteristics of all human languages—encouraging the children to make informed guesses on the subject. Then we shall consider the role of language in the organization of the early human group and the effectiveness it might add to such group activities as hunting. To go from this point to a consideration of myth and its nature is not a difficult step.

It is plain that language can occupy the whole of a year—or two or three. Some teachers may want to devote much time to language, or little, and we hope to make it possible for them to do either. Whether a teacher wishes to concentrate the language material or to distribute it among the other sections is, we believe, a matter of taste, and we hope to design the material in a way that makes both approaches possible. But above all, we hope to provide material and exercises that stimulate a livelier sense of the distinctively human nature of human language.

TOOL MAKING

One starts with several home truths about children and tools. Our children have usually not used many of them, and do not find them of much interest. This may derive from the deeper truth that, in general, children (like their urban parents) think of tools as objects to be bought in hardware stores. Children in our technologically mature society usually have little notion of the relation between tools and our way of life. Production takes place in factories where they have never been, and its products are so packaged as to minimize or cosmetize the production process that brought them into being.

Our section on tools is animated, first of all, by a philosophical approach to the nature of tool using. What is most characteristic of any kind of tool using is not the tools themselves, but rather the program that guides their use. It is in this broader sense that tools take on their proper meaning as amplifiers of human capacities and implementers of human activity.

Seen as amplifiers, tools can be conceived to fall into three general classes—amplifiers of sensory capacities, of motor capacities, and of ratiocinative capacities. Within each type there are many subspecies. There are sensory amplifiers, like microscopes and hearing aids, that are "magnifiers," others, like spirit levels and bobs, that are "reference markers," and so on. Some implement systems "stretch out" time (slow motion cinematography) and others condense it (time-lapse registration). In the realm of motor amplifiers, some tools bind things together, some separate them, some only steady the hand—one of our pupils described a draughtsman's compass as a "steadying tool." And, of course, there are the "soft tools" of ratiocination such as mathematics and logic and the "hard tools" they make possible, ranging from the abacus to the high-speed digital computer and the automaton.

Once we think of tools as imbedded in a program of use— as implementers of human activity—then it becomes possible to deal with the basic idea of substitutability, an idea as crucial to tools as it is to language. If one cannot use or find a certain word or phrase, another near-equivalent can be substituted.

So too with tools: if a skilled carpenter happens not to have brought his chisel to the job, he can usually use something else in its place—the edge of a plane blade, a pocket knife, a sharp stone. In short, tools are not fixed, and the "functional fixedness" found by so many psychologists studying problem solving comes because so much thinking about tools fixes them to convention—a hammer is for nails and nothing but nails.

Our ultimate object in teaching about tools is, as noted before, not so much to explicate tools and their significance as to explore how tools affected man's evolution and still affect his life. In other essays of this volume we have commented on natural selection, how it favored the user of improvised pebble tools and how, in time, survival depended increasingly on the capacity to use and make tools. There are many fascinating concomitants to this story. Better weapons meant a shift to carnivorousness. This in turn led to leisure—or at least less roaming after roots—which in turn made possible permanent or semipermanent settlement. Throughout, changes in tools meant changes in way of life, changes in culture and social organization, changes finally in child rearing (as in the invention of the school).

All of these matters are now challengingly documented by excavations in South Africa and East Africa. We hope to get our pupils to speculate on the changes in a society that accompany these early changes in technology, to get across the idea that a technology requires a counterpart in social organization before it can be used effectively by a society.

Some interesting exercises are being worked out to give a more vivid sense of what tools are. One calls for the taking of a "census of skills"—the tasks that children know how to perform—along with some effort to examine how they were learned (including tool skills). Another revolves around trying to design a tool, so that the children can have some notion of the programmatic questions one asks. The tool in question is an orange peeler (defined narrowly), but more generally the question is how one skins anything. The first attempt in a class produced devices (and ideas) that the children thought superior to anything comparable to be found in the kitchen at home.

There will be some treatment of tools to make tools to make tools, as well as of tools that control various forms of natural power. A possible route into this discussion is an overview of the evolution of tool making generally—from the first "spontaneous" or picked-up tools, to the shaped ones, to those shaped to a pattern, to modern conceptions of man-machine relations, as in contemporary systems research. Indeed, we are trying to devise a game of tool design involving variables such as cost, time, specificity of function, skill required, with the object of making clear the programmatic nature of tools and the manner in which tools represent selective extensions of human powers.

SOCIAL ORGANIZATION

The section on social organization has as its objective to make children aware that there is a structure in a society and that this structure is not fixed once for all. It is structured in the sense that you cannot change one part of the society without changing other parts with it. The way a society arranges itself for carrying out its affairs depends upon a variety of factors, ranging from its ecology at one end to the irreversible course of its history and world view at the other.

A first task is to lead children to recognize explicitly certain basic patterns in a concrete society, patterns they know well in an implicit, intuitive way but which require some special underlining to make them explicit. We plan to use a variety of means to achieve this end.

We should like children to infer from concrete cases that, within most human groups beyond the immediate family, continuity depends not so much upon specific people as upon "roles" filled by people: again, as with language and tool use, there are structures with substitutability. Such social organization is marked by reciprocity and exchange—cooperation is compensated by protection, service by fee, and so on. There is always giving and getting. There are, moreover, forms of legitimacy and sanction that define the limits of possible behavior in any given role. They are the bounds set by a society, and do not depend upon the individual's choice. Law is the classic case, but not the only one. One cannot commit theft legally; but then, too, one cannot ignore friends with impunity, and law has nothing to do with it. A society, moreover, has a certain world view, a way of defining what is "real," what is "good," what is "possible." To this matter we turn in a later section, mentioning it here only because it is one of the ideas we hope to introduce in this part of the course.

We believe these matters can be presented to children in a fashion that is gripping, close to life, and intellectually honest. The pedagogy is still not clear, but we are on the track of some interesting approaches. The difficulty with social organization is its ubiquity and familiarity. Contrast may be our best way of saving social organization from obviousness—by comparing our own forms of social organization with those of baboon troops, of Eskimos, of Bushmen, of prehistoric men as inferred from excavated living floors in Europe and Africa. But beyond this we have now developed a family of games designed to bring social organization into the personal consciousness of the children.

The first of these games, "Hunting," is designed to simulate conditions in an early human group engaged in hunting, and is patterned on the life and ecology of the Bushmen of the Kalahari desert. The game simulates (in the manner of so-called Pentagon games used for increasing the sensitivities of generals) the problem of planning how far one wishes to go in search of various kinds of game, how resources need to be shared by a group to go beyond "varmint" hunting to larger game, how differentiation of labor can come about in weapon making and weapon using, how one must decide among different odds in hunting in one terrain or another. Given the form of the game, its content can be readily varied to fit the conditions of life of other hunting groups, such as the Eskimos, again with the object of contrast.

What has proved particularly interesting in our early work with this game is that it permits the grouping of a considerable amount of "real" material around it—accounts of the life of the Kalahari Bushmen (of which there is an extraordinarily rich record both on film and in written form), their myths and art, the forbidding desert ecology that is their environment. And so too with the Eskimos, for we are in possession of an equally rich documentation on the Netsilik Eskimos of Pelly Bay.

Another approach to social organization is through the concept of the family, particularly the extended family and the general idea of classificatory kinship. We have devised exercises that involve first the "representation" of one's own family by models made of blocks of balsa wood and dowels, all to be shaped and colored as needed. Ten-year-olds have idiosyncratic ways of conceiving of their families, far from the "up-down, right-left" representations of the kinship chart and genealogy. From their own family they go to a "generalized" family, a representation carried out jointly rather than individually. Once they are armed with a new and more ordered mode of picturing an extended family, the lessons then move to a Bushman village and its three generations, with its avoidance patterns, joking relationships, revealing kin terms, and the rest. The children delight in playing "clue" games in which they have to identify who it is on a kinship chart that is being described by such clues as "She makes jokes with Koko." From such kinship analysis one goes easily to division of labor and so on into the fabric of Bushman society.

Finally, and again by contrast, there now exists a vast store of material on the social organization of higher primates—a considerable portion of which is also on film—that serves extremely well to provoke discussion on what is uniquely human about human social organization.

CHILD REARING

The section on child rearing pursues three general themes, in the hope of clarifying them by reference to particular materials in the areas of language, of social organization, of tool making, and of childhood generally. One general theme is the extent to which and the manner in which the long human childhood (assisted as it is by language) leads to the dominance of sentiment in human life, in contrast to the instinctual patterns of gratification and response found to predominate at levels below man. That is to say, affect is aroused and controlled by symbols—human beings have an attitude about anger rather than just anger or not anger. The long process of sentiment formation requires both an extended childhood and access through language to a symbolized culture. Without sentiment (or values or whatever term one prefers) it is highly unlikely that human society or anything like it would be possible.

A second theme is organized around the human (perhaps primate) tendency toward mastery of skill for its own sake—the tendency of the human being, in his learning of the environment, to go beyond immediate adaptive necessity toward innovation. Recent work on human development has underlined this drive for competence. It is present in human play, in the increased variability of human behavior when things get under control. Just as William James commented three-quarters of a century ago that habit was the flywheel of society, we can now say that the innovative urge is the accelerator.

The third theme concerns the shaping of the man by the patterning of his childhood—the fact that, while all humans are intrinsically human, the expression of their humanity is affected by the manner of childhood they have experienced.

The working out of these themes has only begun. One exercise is to get children to describe differences between infancy, childhood, and adulthood for different species—using live specimens brought to class in the case of nonhuman species, siblings for the human species. The specimens for study can be rendered on film; yet the success of a session, say, with a live ten-day-old stub-tailed macaque suggests that the real thing should be used when possible. Various films are in preparation, however, on baboon, macaque, Bushman, and Eskimo childhood.

The effort to teach the unit on childhood has taught us how useful is the concept of the life cycle and how much can be gained by comparing the life cycles of different species and different peoples. It provides, as it were, a matrix in which the facts of growth take on a deeper meaning for children.

WORLD VIEW

The fifth section is concerned with man's drive to explain and represent his world. While it concerns itself with myth, with art, with primitive legend, it is only incidentally designed to provide the stories, the religious images, and the mythic account of man's origins. It would be more accurate to describe the subject as "beginning philosophy" in both senses of that expression — philosophy at the beginning as well as philosophy for young beginners.

Our central conception is that men everywhere are humans, however advanced or "primitive" their civilization. The difference is not one of being more or less human, but of how particular human societies express their human capacities.

A remark by the French anthropologist Lévi-Strauss puts it well:

Prevalent attempts to explain alleged differences between the so-called primitive mind and scientific thought have resorted to qualitative differences between the working processes of the mind in both cases, while assuming that the entities which they were studying remained very much the same. If our interpretation is correct, we are led toward a completely different view—namely, that the kind of logic in mythical thought is as rigorous as that of modern science, and that the difference lies, not in the quality of the intellectual process, but in the nature of things to which it is applied. This is well in agreement with the situation known to prevail in the field of technology: What makes a steel ax superior to a stone ax is not that the first one is better made than the second. They are equally well made, but steel is quite different from stone. In the same way we may be able to show that the same logical processes operate in myth as in science, and that man has always been thinking equally well; the improvement lies, not in the alleged progress of man's mind, but in the discovery of new areas to which it may apply its unchanged and unchanging powers.[1]

At first glance, it may seem that Lévi-Strauss takes a position that is at variance with the view expressed earlier—that tools amplify the powers of muscle, sense, and mind, and the more powerful the tools, the better the amplification. But the difference is on the surface. The great step forward is in the act of linking human powers to expression through tools. Man gains better technical control of his world through modern science than he does through mythic explanation; but in science and in myth the same component processes or logical operations provide the base. It is in this sense that we try to make clear that man is equally human whether he uses a stone ax or a steel one, explains eclipses by astronomy or by spirits, murders with a gun or by the use of magic.

[1] Claude Lévi-Strauss, *Structural Anthropology,* trans. by Claire Jacobson and Brooke Grundfest Schoepf (New York: Basic Books, 1963), p. 230.

All cultures are created equal. One society—say, that of the Eskimo—may have only a few tools, but they are used in a versatile way. The woman's knife does what our scissors do, but it also serves to scrape hides, clean and thin them, and so on. The man's knife is used for killing and skinning animals, carving wood and bone, cutting snow for building blocks for the igloo, chopping meat into bites. Such simple weapons are "the mother of tools," from which by specialization a number of tools derive. What is lost in variety is won in versatility.

So too with symbolic systems. The very essence of being human lies in the use of symbols. We do not know what the hierarchy of primacy is among speech, song, dance, and drawing, but, whichever came first, as soon as it stood for something else than the act itself, man was born; as soon as it caught on with another man, culture was born; and as soon as there were two symbols, a system was born. A dance, a song, a painting, and a narrative can all symbolize the same thing. They do so differently. One way of searching for the structure of a world view is to take an important narrative and see what it ultimately tells. A narrative, or at least a corpus of narratives, may be what philosophy used to be. It may reflect what is believed about the celestial bodies and their relation to man; it may tell how man came into being, how social life was founded, what is believed about death and about life after death; it may codify law and morals. In short, it may give expression to the group's basic tenets on astronomy, theology, sociology, law, education, even aesthetics.

In studying symbolic systems, we want the students to understand myths rather than to learn them. We will give them examples from simple cultures for the same reason that the anthropologist travels into an isolated society. Our hope is to lead the children to understand how man goes about explicating his world, making sense of it, and that one kind of explanation is no more human than another.

We have selected, for our starting point, two hunting-gathering societies—Eskimo and Bushman—to show what the life experience of hunting peoples is. From the scrutiny of the myths of these groups, it is immediately clear that you can tell a society by its narratives. The ecology, the economy, the social structure, the tasks of men and women, and their fears and anxieties are reflected in the stories, and in a way that the children can handle. One good example of Eskimo narrative or Eskimo poetry, if skillfully handled in class, can show the child that the problems of an Eskimo are like our problems: to cope with his environment, to cope with his fellow men, and to cope with himself. We hope to show that wherever man lives, he manages not only to survive and to breed, but also to think and to express his thoughts. But we can also let the children enjoy the particulars of a given culture—the sense of an alien ecology, whether the bush or ice and snow—and gain an empathic understanding for alien styles.

We introduce an origin myth, of things taking their present order, the sun shining over the paths of the Bushmen, and the Bushmen starting to hunt. But we should suggest some possible theories to make the discussion profitable, theories not in words, but in ways of reading and understanding a myth. If the narrative is called a myth, the state of things it deals with is radically different from the way things are now, and these differences are worth examining. It is possible to devise ways for children to analyze a plot. If done with one story variant only, such an analysis may yield something akin to a phrase-structure grammar; if done with a group of myths, something comparable to a transformational grammar. It is intriguing to see how stories change. Children sense the structure of narratives intuitively and can be helped to appreciate them more powerfully.

Why should the structure of myth be taught so early? Why not postpone it until the student can handle the "theory" itself, not only the examples? There is a reason: if such things are new to a twenty-year-old, there is not only a new view to learn, but an old established view to unlearn. We want the children to recognize that man is constantly seeking to bring reason into his world, that he does so with a variety of symbolic tools, and that he does so with a striking and fully rational humanity. It is a big order, but worth the try.

But it is also necessary that the children "feel" myth as well as understand it—for it is different from "explanation" or "narrative." We have found that this requires much care in the teaching. At least two methods have been used, each with what seemed to be striking effect in gripping the children's imagination. In one, a week-long conference, the children are introduced abruptly to Eskimo society by a film of the family of Zachary, Marta, and their four-year-old son Alexei (a family that is followed through the year by our films shot at Pelley Bay). It is one in which they are jigging through the spring ice for salmon, and catching a good share, until a howling gale rises and the film comes to a close. It is particularly useful as an "introduction" to Netsilik life, at once full of humanity and the wildness of the terrain and weather. There follows an extended discussion of seals, and how much of what they wore and lived in and used in daily life was derived from the seal. Following this, there is a short film of Zachary, technically extraordinary, stalking a seal on the ice, creeping up on it slowly and with evident guile, hoping to harpoon it before it can get back into the water through its breathing hole. Zachary fails. The children try their hand at writing a dream that he might have that night. They need a fair amount of encouraging to avoid the "slick" dream pattern of the mass media. Why did Zachary miss? With his beautiful skill and tools and experience, why did the seal get away? Let the dream be about that. The stories and illustrations are sometimes startling, very often "mythlike," always dramatic. Only after these are the children introduced to Nuliajik, the myth of the origin of seals, the Eskimo orphan girl who tried to climb on the raft and was refused, her fingers cut off and turned to seals, and left with an ever unfulfilled sense of vengeance against humanity, holding back the seals over whom she exercised dominion.

We were struck by how strongly the children sensed the mythic qualities of the Nuliajik tale, how much (through their own efforts) they had become adept at judging an imaginative "explanation." Some still preferred their own stories to Nuliajik, but no matter. The exercise in question, having been carried out in a hurried summer session, might have been carried further to include what another class had done—constructing "stories that include opposites," exercises to elucidate the formal structure of myths. The children first made a long list of opposites: cold-warm, man-woman, brave-scared, and so on. They then chose one or as many as they wished from the list to write about, to "reconcile" or "get together." They were absorbed by the task and, in the process, developed a deeper sense of what a myth is, discovering by their own efforts at composition what, by other analytic exercises, they were also able to discover about a corpus of Netsilik myths that they had been reading.

PEDAGOGY

The most persistent problem in social studies is to rescue the phenomena of social life from familiarity, without at the same time making it all seem "primitive" and bizarre. Four techniques are proving particularly useful in achieving this end. The first is contrast, of which much has already been said. The second is the stimulation and use of informed guessing, hypothesis making, conjectural procedures. The third is participation—particularly by the use of games that incorporate the formal properties of the phenomena for which the game is an analogue. In this sense, a game is like a mathematical model —an artificial but often powerful representation of reality. The fourth is the ancient approach of stimulating self-consciousness. We believe there is a learnable strategy for discovering one's unspoken notions, one's unstated ways of approaching things.

Before considering each of these let me say a word about a point of view quite different from ours. It holds that one should begin teaching social studies by presenting the familiar world of home, the street, and the neighborhood. It is a thoroughly commendable ideal; its only fault is its failure to recognize how difficult it is for human beings to see generality in what has become familiar. The friendly postman is indeed the vicar of federal powers, but to lead the child to the recognition of such powers requires many detours into the realm of what constitutes power, federal or other, and how, for example, constituted power and willfully exercised force differ. We would rather find a way of stirring the curiosity of the children with particulars whose intrinsic drama and human significance are plain, whether close at hand or at a far remove. If we can concurrently activate a passion for bringing order into what has been studied, the task is well started.

A word first about contrast. Its use in pedagogy is ancient, and so is its place in learning theory as an important factor in establishing conceptual categories. We hope to use four principal sources of contrast: man versus higher primates, man versus prehistoric man, contemporary technological man versus primitive man, and man versus child. We have been gathering materials relevant to each of the contrasts—film, stories, artifacts, readings, pictures, and, above all, ideas for pointing up contrasts in the interest of achieving clarity.

Indeed, we hope to achieve for our pupils a sense of continuity by first presenting them with what seems like contrast and letting them live with it long enough to sense wherein what before seemed bizarrely different is, in fact, closely akin to things they understand from their own lives. So it is particularly with our most extensive collection of material, a film record, taken through the full cycle of the year, of a family of Netsilik Eskimo. The ecology and the externals are full of contrast to daily life in an American or European setting. But there is enough material available so that our pupils can work into the year's cycle of a single family and get a sense of the integrity not only of a family, but of a culture. It is characteristic of Netsilik Eskimos, for example, that they make a few beautifully specialized tools and weapons, such as their fishing lester or spear. But it is also apparent that each man can make do with the stones he finds around him, that the Eskimo is a superbly gifted *bricoleur*. Whenever he needs to do something, improvised tools come from nowhere. A flat stone, a little fish oil, a touch of arctic cotton, and he has a lamp. So while the Eskimo footage provides a sharp contrast to modern technological man, it serves perhaps ever better to present the inherent, internal logic of a society, any society. Each has its own approach to technology, to the use of intelligence. It is in the recognition of this unique integrity in human society—wherever it is found—that children are led from what first seemed like contrast to what is finally seen as continuity.

About the hypothetical mode, I think I can sum up our attitude by saying that it avails little to give information that is not asked for. Let me illustrate. We have a film of Zachary, the father of the Netsilik Eskimo family we have filmed, hunting seal alone by waiting for the seal to come to the surface of a breathing hole in the ice. A seal has about a dozen breathing holes. Which one to stalk? And if the hunting party were six in number, how distribute them? In fact, we have film of a group hunting seal by watching the breathing holes. But before we show it, we like to get the children figuring out the problem on their own. So too with the organization of a baboon troop of adult males, adult females, juveniles, and infants. How do they arrange themselves to get through territory where there are predators? It is far more interesting to learn the facts *after* one has tried to figure them out for oneself.

Games go a long way toward getting children involved in understanding language, social organization, and the rest; they also introduce, as we have already noted, the idea of a theory of these phenomena. We do not know to what extent these games will be successful, but we shall give them a careful try. They provide a superb means of getting children to participate actively in the process of learning—as players rather than spectators.

As for stimulating self-consciousness about thinking and its ways, we feel that the best approach is through mastering the art of getting and using information—learning what is involved in going beyond the information given and what makes it possible to take such leaps. Richard Crutchfield has produced results in this sphere using nothing more complicated than a series of comic books in which the adventures of a detective, aided by his nephew and niece, are recounted. The theme is using clues cleverly. As children explore the implications of clues encountered, their general reasoning ability increases, and they formulate more and better hypotheses. We plan to design materials in which children have an opportunity to do this sort of thinking with questions related to the course —possibly in connection with prehistoric materials, where it will be most relevant. If it turns out to be the case that the clothing that people wore was made from the skin of the ibex, what can they infer about the size of a hunting party and how would they look for data?

Children should be at least as self-conscious about their strategies of thought as they are about their attempts to commit things to memory. They should be conscious, too, of the tools of thought—causal explanation, categorization, and the rest.

One of those tools—perhaps the principal one—is language, and we shall try to get the children to have a look at it in this light.

The most urgent need of all is to give our pupils the experience of what it is to use a theoretical model, with some sense of what is involved in being aware that one is trying out a theory. We shall be using a fair number of rather sophisticated theoretical notions; they will be intuitively presented rather than formally stated, to be sure, but they will help to give children the experience of using alternative models.

We shall, of course, try to encourage students to discover on their own. Children need not discover all generalizations for themselves, obviously. Yet we want to give them opportunity to develop a decent competence at it and a proper confidence in their ability to operate independently. There is also some need for the children to pause and review in order to recognize the connections within what they have learned— the kind of internal discovery that is probably of highest value. The cultivation of such a sense of connectedness is surely the heart of the matter. For if we do nothing else, we should somehow give to children a respect for their own powers of thinking, for their power to generate good questions, to come up with interesting informed guesses. So much of social studies till now has been a congeries of facts. We should like to make the study more rational, more amenable to the use of mind in the large rather than mere memorizing.

THE FORM OF THE COURSE

It is quite plain that the success of any course depends upon how well it is handled by a teacher, and this is particularly so in social studies, where the attitude of the teacher speaks as eloquently as any materials in the course itself. We are mindful of the problem and are trying to deal with it by the nature of the guides we are providing teachers. For it is one thing to describe the nature of a course in terms of its underlying discipline and its pedagogical aims, and quite another to render these hopes into a workable form for real teachers in real classes. Teachers are sufficiently constrained by their work loads so that it would be vain to hope they might read generally and widely enough in the field to be able to give form to the course in their own terms. The materials to be covered in this particular course, moreover, are so vast in scope as to be forbidding. The materials, in short, have got to be made usable and attractive not only to the highly gifted teacher, but to teachers in general, and to teachers who live with the ordinary fatigue of coping with younger pupils day by day. They cannot be overburdened with reading, nor can the reading be of such an order as to leave them with a feeling of impotence. At the same time, the material presented should be loosely enough woven to permit the teacher to satisfy his interests in forming a final product to be presented to children.

That much said, we can state what we mean by *units*, the elements of which the course is made. A unit is a body of materials and exercises that may occupy as much as several days of class time or as little as half a class period. In short, it can be played to the full and consume a considerable amount of the course content, or be taken *en passant*. Indeed, some units will surely be skipped and are intended only for those teachers who have a special interest in a topic or a particular kind of exercise. There will be more units than can possibly be fitted into a year's course, and teachers will be encouraged to put them together in a form that is commodious to their own intent.

In a manner of speaking, a collection of such units constitutes a course of study. But the image is unfortunate, connoting as it does so many beads strung together by some principle of succession. It is our hope that after a certain number of units have been got through, a unit can then be introduced to "recode" what has gone before, to exploit connection. Some units only review and present no new material.

A master unit sits on the teacher's ready shelf, and consists of six constituent elements.

1. *Talks to teachers.* These consist of lively accounts of the nature of the unit—particularly the nature of its mystery, what about it impels curiosity and wonder. Our experience in preparing these indicates the importance of staying close to the great men in the field, if possible to find a great article that can be presented in somewhat abridged form. The design of a language (taken from Hockett) or the nature of kinship (taken from Radcliffe-Brown) or how a thing should be called (Roger Brown)—these are examples. The genre needs further study and we are exploring the kind of writing required—something that is at once science and poetry. If it should turn out that a student finds "talks to teachers" worth reading, so much the better.

2. *Queries and contrasts.* In trying out materials to be taught, we have learned certain ways of getting ideas across or getting the students to think out matters on their own. Often these can be embodied in devices—pictures, reading, and diagrams. But sometimes they are best stated as hints to teachers about questions to use and contrasts to invoke.

"How could you improve the human hand?" turns out to be a useful question. So does the question, "What are the different ways something can 'stand for' something else, like a red light 'standing for' *stop?*"

We have already spoken of our tactical fondness for contrasts, and we are coming up with useful ones in our designing. One such is to have students contrast a cry of pain with the words, "It hurts." Another is to compare the usual words from which phonemes may be inferred, like hit, hat, hate, hut, hot. Or the difference to be found in the two allophones of the phoneme /p/ in the words *spit* and *pit*—the latter of which will blow out a match held to the lips, the former not—although the two are regarded as the "same letter" or the "same sound," whereas *hat* and *hate* are "different."

3. *Devices.* This part of the unit contains the "stuff"—the material for students. Principal among the devices is, of course, reading material, and we are, like others, struggling to get such material prepared. In good season we hope to understand this obscure matter better. Currently, we are operating, much as others have, to find, or cause to be written, material that is interesting, informative, and in a decent style.

But there are many devices beyond reading that are in need of developing for different units. One is the film loop for use with the Technicolor cartridge projectors that we use increasingly. We are putting together four-minute loops constructed from Eskimo, Bushman, and baboon footage, with the intention of *asking* questions or *posing* riddles. Too often, films have a way of producing passivity. Can we devise ones to do the opposite? Why did *Last Year at Marienbad* abrade the curiosity so well?

We are also exploring what can be done with games, as already noted, and with animation and graphics and maps.

4. *Model exercises.* From time to time in devising a unit it becomes plain that the problem we face is less in the subject matter and more in the intellectual habits of children in ordinary schools. We have commented on some of these problems already—the difficulty many children and not a few adults have in distinguishing necessary from necessary and sufficient conditions, the tendency of children to be lazy in using information, not exploiting its inferential power to nearly the degree warranted, difficulties in categorization.

Model exercises are designed to overcome such intellectual difficulties. We think they are best kept imbedded in the very materials one is teaching. But it is often helpful to provide the teacher with additional special devices. We intend to use puzzles, conundrums, games—a kind of pedagogical first-aid kit.

5. *Documentaries*. These are accounts, or even tape recordings, of ordinary children at work with the materials in the unit. We would like the documentary to be both exemplary and at the same time typical enough to be within reach of a teacher in his own work.

Along with the documentary goes a more analytic description. The analytic documentary is designed to serve two purposes. The first is to make it plainer both to ourselves and to teachers what in fact are the psychological problems involved in particular kinds of intellectual mastery that we hope to stimulate in children. In this sense, the analytic documentary is a further clarification of our pedagogical objectives. But in another sense, it represents an attempt on our part to accustom teachers to thinking in more general terms about the intellectual life of children. The second objective—call it educational—is to provide teachers with what might be a more useful educational psychology than the kind that is found conventionally in textbooks dedicated to that obscure subject.

It is our hope that as we proceed in our work there will be spin-offs in the form of general research problems that can be worked on by research centers not directly geared to the daily routines of curriculum building and curriculum testing. The work of such centers, as well as research in the regular literature on intellectual development, will constitute a continuing font from which we can draw material for the analytic documentaries.

6. *Supplementary materials*. The final section of the unit "kit" consists of such supplementary materials as paperbacks (and lists of related paperbacks), additional film and game materials, and other devices that might attract the attention of either a diligent student or an aspiring teacher. Without question, it will become clearer what is needed by way of supple-

ment once we have gone further into providing what will be our standard fare. One new type of film has already been discovered to be particularly helpful as supplementary material. In constructing units, we have often brought together the leading scholar who is helping construct materials and a group of pupils who are studying the material. The scholar has been "there"—whether Professor Asen Balikci with the Eskimos, Dr. Richard Lee or Lorna Marshall with the Bushmen, Dr. Irven DeVore with East African baboons—and the children have read and pondered. What ensues is a colloquy in which children and scholar alike show how lively and direct a discourse is possible.

If we were totally successful in planning and teaching the course, we would have achieved five ideals:

1. To give our pupils respect for and confidence in the powers of their own mind.

2. To extend that respect and confidence to their power to think about the human condition, man's plight, and his social life.

3. To provide a set of workable models that make it simpler to analyze the nature of the social world in which we live and the condition in which man finds himself.

4. To impart a sense of respect for the capacities and humanity of man as a species.

5. To leave the student with a sense of the unfinished business of man's evolution.

Chapter 5

Teaching a Native Language

I HAVE OFTEN thought that I would do more for my students by teaching them to write and think in English than teaching them my own subject. It is not so much that I value discourse to others that is right and clear and graceful—be it spoken or written—as that practice in such discourse is the only way of assuring that one says things right and courteously and powerfully *to oneself*. For it is extraordinarily difficult to say foolishness clearly without exposing it for what it is— whether you recognize it yourself or have the favor done you. So let me explore, then, what is involved in the relation between language and thinking, or, better, between writing and thinking. Or perhaps it would be even better to speak of how the use of language affects the use of mind.

Consider this. As between reading, listening, and speaking, one falls asleep most easily reading, next most easily listening, and only with the greatest difficulty while writing or speaking —although I have seen both the latter happen among those deprived of sleep for long periods. There is an important difference between deciphering (as in listening or reading), and enciphering (as in speaking or writing). In listening or reading our span of attention typically lags behind the further- most point where our eye or ear has traveled. We hold words and phrases in mind until we can tie the utterance together. A colleague of mine has been studying the retrospective integrating mechanisms involved in listening, and he finds his subjects holding decisions in abeyance until they see what is coming, which then permits them to go back over what has been said in order to give it a final syntactical rendering. Of course, we aid our auditors and readers by reducing the amount of memorial baggage they carry to the end of a sentence. And so we write:

This is the dog that chased the cat that killed the rat,

and avoid:

This is the rat that the cat that the dog chased killed.

In speaking or writing, the pattern is quite different: the arrow points forward. The speaker or writer rides ahead of rather than behind the edge of his utterance. He is organizing ahead, marshaling thoughts and words and transforming them into utterances, anticipating what requires saying. If the listener is trafficking back and forth between the present and the immediate past, the speaker is principally shuttling between the present and the future. The plight of the listener is to "fall behind"; of the speaker, to "get ahead of himself." Falling behind is a state in which the listener has insufficient processing time for decoding; getting ahead of oneself is a failure to anticipate properly. Pressed for time, the listener falls further and further behind, the speaker gets further and further ahead of himself. It is not surprising, then, that listening is soporific in the sense of blurring the present with the past. The tonic effect of speaking is that one thrusts the edge of the present toward the future. In one case anticipation is forced into abeyance. In the other, it dominates the activity.

You will quite properly have guessed that I am about to urge that reading be rescued from its passivity and turned into a more active enterprise. Indeed, I do believe just that. But it is not a new theme. We have all discovered it (with delight) on our own. As a student, I took a course with I. A. Richards, a beautiful man and a great necromancer. It began with that extraordinary teacher turning his back to the class and writing on the blackboard in his sharply angular hand the lines:

> Gray is all theory;
> Green grows the golden tree of life.

For three weeks we stayed with the lines, with the imagery of the classic and romantic views, with the critics who had sought to explore the two ways of life; we became involved in reading a related but bad play of Goethe's, *Torquato Tasso,* always in a state of dialogue though Richards alone spoke. The reading time for eleven words was three weeks. It was the antithesis of just reading, and the reward in the end was that I owned outright, free and clear, eleven words. A good bargain. Never before had I read with such a lively sense of conjecture, like a speaker and not a listener, or like a writer and not a reader.

I need not argue the virtues of reading oneself awake. Rather, I mean to pose a somewhat different problem, though a closely related one. Let me begin by stating rather baldly— though there is indeed ample evidence to support my point— that language is a major instrument of thought. When we are thinking at the far reach of our capacities, we are engaged with words, even led forward by them. Take the first appearance of syntax in the life of the child. During his second year, he develops that curious but powerful construction, the one-word utterance or holophrase: *mummy, sticky, allgone, no, daddah.* If you study the course of growth, you will discover that on a certain day, and it should be celebrated with an anniversary party each year, the child mysteriously constructs a syntactical utterance. Mother washes jam from his hands. He says, *Allgone sticky.* If you keep observing you will discover further that during the next weeks he drives the new construction to its limit: a syntactic structure composed of a closed pivot class, *allgone,* and an open class that contains practically every other word in his vocabulary. *Allgone* what have you. Soon new pivot words emerge, always in this same kind of privileged position with regard to the other words in his vocabulary. In the first month after their appearance, there will be a few dozen utterances containing a pivot construction. A few months later they will number well over a thousand.

What has this to do with our subject? It has precisely this to do with it: the child has acquired not only a way of saying something but a powerful instrument for combining experiences, an instrument that can now be used as a tool for organizing thoughts about things. It has been remarked that words are invitations to form concepts. It can equally be said that the combinatorial or productive property of language is an invitation to take experience apart and put it together again in new ways. Consider the new-found power and grace of the child we considered a moment ago. He returns from a trip in his stroller: *allgone byebye.* I am urging, in effect, that in some unknown but considerable measure, the power of words is the power of thought. There has been the teaching of English, as it has come to be called in the past half century. But it may well be teaching the calculus of thought as well. Indeed, I should like to urge that the closest kin to the teacher of English composition is the teacher of mathematics. The latter is teaching a somewhat artificialized calculus of thought that applies principally to what are called well-formed problems. The ill-formed problems for which the calculus of grammar is most useful are incalculably more interesting and strenuous. That is what the teacher of composition has in his charge.

How conceive of language as a calculus of thought for ill-formed problems—problems, that is, without unique solutions? I should prefer to look at it from the point of view of the

functions that language serves the speaker outwardly, and
then to consider which of these functions also serve internally
to help us organize our thoughts about things. My distinguished colleague and friend Roman Jakobson has some pen-
etrating comments to make on this subject.[1] He suggests that
there are six discernible functions of language: emotive, conative, referential, metalingual, poetic, and phatic. It is a formidable list. He derives it from the nature of discourse, and if
we assume that much of thought is internalized discourse or
dialogue, it seems reasonable to suppose, does it not, that these
functions should be represented in thinking. Discourse consists, in its essentials, of an *addresser,* an *addressee,* a *contact*
that joins them, a *message* passing between them, a *context*
to which the message refers and a linguistic *code* that governs
the way in which messages are put together and things
referred to. The referential function of language has to do
with the manner in which things are pointed to by utterances.
"That is a man." "What happened to the team spirit?" The
emotive function expresses the internal feelings of the addresser
through words or intonation. "How nice to be here" is a banal
example. "Damn" is better. The conative function seeks to
produce behavior in the addressee. "Get thee to a nunnery,"
or "Please hold my hat." The phatic function has as its aim
the maintenance of contact, and is best illustrated by the
"uh-huh" uttered over the telephone when we wish to make
it clear to the other that we are still there. Opening sentences
between old friends long separated and newly met provide
a treasury of phatic utterances. The poetic function has to do
solely with the message for its own sake. "A girl used to talk
about 'the horrible Harry.' 'Why horrible?' 'Because I hate him.'
'But why not *dreadful, terrible, frightful, disgusting?*' 'I don't
know why, but *horrible* fits him better.' " Jakobson proclaims
triumphantly, and quite correctly, "Without realizing it, she

[1] In T. A. Sebeok, ed., *Style in Language* (New York: John Wiley &
Sons, 1960), pp. 350–374.

clung to the poetic device of paramasia." In the jargon of linguistics, the poetic function shifts the emphasis from rules of word selection to rules of word combination, the pure concern with the structure of the message, the delight of all who care about words. And finally the metalingual. It is jurisprudence applied to language: does this or that utterance fit the code—is or is not "mare" the feminine of "horse," and what is its contrast class? Or simply, "Do you know what I mean?"

I hope I have not bored you with the technicalities of making a single point. The point is, simply, that language serves many functions, pursues many aims, employs many voices. What is most extraordinary of all is that it commands as it refers, describes as it makes poetry, adjudicates as it expresses, creates beauty as it gets things clear, serves all other needs as it maintains contact. It does all these things at once, and does them with a due regard to rules and canons such that a native speaker very early in life is usually able to tell whether they were well done or botched. I would like to suggest that a man of intellectual discipline is one who is master of the various functions of speech, one who has a sense of how to vary them, how to say what he wishes to say—to himself and to others. Too much contact maintenance and too little reference is a bore. Too much expression and too little anything else is a muddle. What is true of external discourse may also be true of internal discourse with oneself. But consider now the relation of external and internal language. Can one be clear to oneself and turbid in saying it?

The shape or style of a mind is, in some measure, the outcome of internalizing the functions inherent in the language we use. Let me illustrate what is meant by internalization by citing two experiments, both by Russian psycholinguists.[2] Each experimenter set a task that was straightforward enough. When

[2] For details, see A. R. Luria, *The Role of Speech in the Regulation of Normal and Abnormal Behavior* (New York: Liveright, 1961).

one kind of display appeared, the young subjects were to press a bulb in their right hand; when the other appeared, the left-handed bulb was to be pressed. In the first experiment, conducted by Martsinovskaya, children between the ages of three and eight were the subjects. Their first task was to press one bulb when a red circle appeared, the other when a green appeared. The circles were presented on either gray or yellow backgrounds. It is an easy task responding to a figure on a ground, and three-year-olds do it as well as the older children. Now, when the task was mastered, the children were told to ignore the red and green figures and respond instead to the backgrounds, one bulb for yellow and the other for gray, regardless of what color figure appeared on them. Under these circumstances, the younger children had great difficulty. They seemed unable to inhibit reactions to the figures, were somehow unable to instruct themselves properly. The older children took it in stride. And now the second experiment, this one carried out by Abramyan, again with children of the same age range. He argued that the difficulty experienced by the younger children in Martsinovskaya's experiment was that they were unable to encode the instructions in internal language in a fashion that would permit them to regulate their own behavior. Their internalized language went no further than concrete declaration. If the instructions could be converted into such a declarative form, then they would succeed. So he repeated the earlier experiment with only one variation: he substituted airplane silhouettes for the circles in the original experiment. Now when the child had to shift from figure to ground they were able to say, "Airplanes can fly on sunny days—yellow background; but they cannot fly on cloudy days—gray background. Press with one hand when the airplanes can fly, with the other when they cannot." With this small change, the three-year-olds could perform quite as well as the eights. Language, in short, provides an internal technique for programming our discriminations, our behavior, our forms of awareness. If there is suitable internal language, the task can be done.

This is a very simple, perhaps too simple, experiment. It does, however, raise a deep question about the relation between being able to do or think something on the one hand and being able to say it to oneself on the other. That there is some intimate relationship is quite plain, though it is equally plain that we are only beginning to understand the nature of that relationship. The Chinese proverb can sometimes be reversed, and there are instances in which a single word is worth a thousand pictures—the word "implosion" was classified top secret by the Manhattan Project during the war. But words have limits. When we follow Mr. MacLeish in admitting that a poem is mute, what we are saying, I suspect, is that words do not fully exhaust the knowledge and sensibility contained in our acts and our images.

I am not urging that the word is the summit of all intellectual discipline and cultivation. Rather, I would suggest that the way of language in knowing is the most powerful means we have for performing transformations on the world, for transmuting its shape by recombination in the interest of possibility. I commented earlier that there should be a special birthday to celebrate the entrance of the child into the human race, dated from the moment when he first uses combinatorial grammar. Each of the functions of language has its combinatorial necromancy, its enormous productiveness. It is with the cultivation of these combinatorial powers that I am concerned.

Now let me return to instruction in one's native language and the degree to which it may also be instruction in the use of the implements of thought. Let me exaggerate. If there is not a developed awareness of the different functions that language serves, the resulting affliction will be not only lopsided speaking and writing, but a lopsided mind. Like the children in the two experiments, the afflicted person will be

restricted in his coping to events for which his stunted language
provides suitable equipment. And one day he may be forced
to fight a forest fire with a water pistol.

But how does one achieve awareness, mastery, and finesse
in the various functions to which language is devoted? How
indeed does one become masterfully adept at the rules for
forming functionally appropriate utterances for the consumption of others or for one's own consumption, *save by exercise?*
Many of us have delighted over the years in the weekend com-
petitions of the *New Statesman.* "Write the Declaration of
Independence in the style of the Old Testament." Or, "Do a
prose rendering of the 'Charge of the Light Brigade' in the
style of Henry James." There is a comparable delight in
Max Beerbohm's *Christmas Garland* or Raymond Queneau's
Exercises in Style. To write in different styles and in different
voices—a beseeching account of evolution, an expressive account of Newton's Law of Moments, whatever—surely this is
one right path.

I confess to having achieved one minor success in the teaching of English. The pupil was one of my own children. Several
years ago she was applying for entry to a college that requires
applicants to write an autobiographical sketch. She wrote one
and brought the piece to me for comment. It was very much
her—full of her warm enthusiasm—and yet the written document was almost a caricature of a warm-hearted girl. It is
difficult to be graceful in one's comments about another's
writing, and the more so when there is a close bond between
critic and his charge. You cannot say to a seventeen-year-old
girl, however gay your tone of voice, "My dear, this is gushy."
The diagnosis of gushiness carries no remedial prescription
with it. I stumbled on the happy formula. Could she rewrite
the piece without a single adjective, not a one? Two hours
later she returned with the news that her first draft had been
disgustingly effusive, that I should have told her so, and that in

spite of my failure in candor the sketch was being rescued from its original state. I suspect something more happened than just a change in writing.

It is the case that the skills of speaking and listening precede those of reading and writing. Why does writing come so hard to the schoolchild? There is often a lag of from six to eight years between his "linguistic age" in writing and in speaking. Written speech is obviously a quite different enterprise from oral speech. The brilliant Russian psychologist Vygotsky suggested that writing and reading are second-order abstractions. In spoken speech there is more likely to be not only a referent present, but a great amount of steering provided by the social demands of the dialogue. Written speech may bear the same relation to spoken speech that algebra bears to arithmetic. A written word stands for a spoken word used in any context whatever. A spoken word "stands for" a thing or state or thought—not another word in a different medium. In written language, moreover, no interlocutor is presupposed and none is there. Spoken utterances are normally determined in large part by the demands of a dialogue, with the interlocutor helping frame our decisions about what requires saying. Whoever uses written speech must detach himself from immediate social interaction altogether and conjure up in his own mind a situation appropriate to the written words with which he is dealing.

Let me suggest, then, that by virtue of its very separation from immediate dialogue, the act of writing creates a new awareness about the nature and powers of language. But if this is so, why is it that a man through his entire life as *Homo scribens* will continue to write with no improvement in his sense of craft and little improvement in his use of mind? It may well be that to become aware of what one has written requires that one hear it, listen to it, compare the spoken with the written version. Perhaps the paraphernalia of the "language laboratory" should be used, if only to have students read their compositions to a tape and then suffer the tape to read back aloud what they have written. There should be a tutor nearby, doubtless, to correct and encourage. But I am hard put to know what he would say to his charge. I would rather have the tutor play another role—not at the student's elbow but speaking from the tape. Let him take the student's composition and rewrite it in various styles, each capitalizing on different functions of language and on different techniques of saying or organizing what the student said. Then let the student write some more and listen, listen, listen.

It was Dante, I believe, who commented that the poor workman hated his tools. It is more than a little troubling to me that so many of our students dislike two of the major tools of thought—mathematics and the conscious deployment of their native language in its written form, both of them devices for ordering thoughts about things and thoughts about thoughts. I should hope that in the new era that lies ahead we will give a proper consideration to making these tools more lovable. Perhaps the best way to make them so is to make them more powerful in the hands of their users.

Chapter 6

The Will
To Learn

THE SINGLE MOST characteristic thing about human beings is that they learn. Learning is so deeply ingrained in man that it is almost involuntary, and thoughtful students of human behavior have even speculated that our specialization as a species is a specialization for learning. For, by comparison with organisms lower in the animal kingdom, we are ill equipped with prepared reflex mechanisms. As William James put it decades ago, even our instinctive behavior occurs only once, thereafter being modified by experience. With a half century's perspective on the discoveries of Pavlov, we know that man not only is conditioned by his environment, but may be so conditioned even against his will.

Why then invoke the idea of a "will to learn"? The answer derives from the idea of education, a human invention that takes a learner beyond "mere" learning. Other species begin their learning afresh each generation, but man is born into a culture that has as one of its principal functions the conservation and transmission of past learning. Given man's physical characteristics, indeed, it would be not only wasteful but probably fatal for him to reinvent even the limited range of technique and knowledge required for such a species to survive in the temperate zone. This means that man cannot depend upon a casual process of learning; he must be "educated." The young human must regulate his learning and his attention by reference to external requirements. He must eschew what is vividly right under his nose for what is dimly in a future that is often incomprehensible to him. And he must do so in a strange setting where words and diagrams and other abstractions suddenly become very important. School demands an orderliness and neatness beyond what the child has known before; it requires restraint and immobility never asked of him before; and often it puts him in a spot where he does not *know* whether he knows and can get no indication from anybody for minutes at a time as to whether he is on the right track. Perhaps most important of all, school is away from home with all that fact implies in anxiety, or challenge, or relief.

In consequence of all this the problem of "the will to learn" becomes important, indeed exaggerated. Let us not delude ourselves: it is a problem that cannot be avoided, though it can be made manageable, I think. We shall explore what kinds of factors lead to satisfaction in "educated" learning, to pleasure in the practice of learning as it exists in the necessarily artificial atmosphere of the school. Almost all children possess what have come to be called "intrinsic" motives for learning. An intrinsic motive is one that does not depend upon reward that lies outside the activity it impels. Reward inheres in the successful termination of that activity or even in the activity itself.

Curiosity is almost a prototype of the intrinsic motive. Our attention is attracted to something that is unclear, unfinished, or uncertain. We sustain our attention until the matter in hand becomes clear, finished, or certain. The achievement of clarity or merely the search for it is what satisfies. We would think it preposterous if somebody thought to reward us with praise or profit for having satisfied our curiosity. However pleasant such external reward might be, and however much we might come to depend upon it, the external reward is something added. What activates and satisfies curiosity is something inherent in the cycle of activity by which we express curiosity. Surely such activity is biologically relevant, for curiosity is essential to the survival not only of the individual but of the species. There is considerable research that indicates the extent to which even nonhuman primates will put forth effort for a chance to encounter something novel on which to exercise curiosity. But it is clear that unbridled curiosity is little more than unlimited distractibility. To be interested in everything that comes along is to be interested in nothing for long. Studies of the behavior of three-year-olds, for example, indicate the degree to which they are dominated from the outside by the parade of vivid impressions that pass their way. They turn to this bright color, that sharp sound, that new shiny surface. Many ends are beyond their reach, for they cannot sustain a steady course when the winds shift. If anything, they are "too curious." They live by what psychologists have long called the laws of primary attention: attention dominated by vividness and change in the environment. There has been much speculation about the function of this early and exhausting tempo of curiosity. One neuropsychologist, Donald Hebb, has suggested that the child is drinking in the world, better to construct his neural "models" of the environment. And it is plain that a stunted organism is produced by depriving an infant of the rich diet of impressions on which his curiosity normally feeds with such extravagance. Animals raised in homogenized environments show crippling deficits in their later ability to learn and to transfer what they have learned. Children "kept in the attic" by misguided or psychotic parents show the same striking backwardness. Indeed, even the children who have suffered the dull, aseptic environment of backward foundling homes often show a decline in intelligence that can be compensated only by vigorous measures of enrichment. So surely, then, an important early function is served by the child's omnivorous capacity for new impressions. He is sorting the world, storing those things that have some recurrent regularity and require "knowing," discriminating them from the parade of random impressions.[1]

But if attention is to be sustained, directed to some task and held there in spite of temptations that come along, then obviously constraints must be established. The voluntary deployment of curiosity, so slowly and painfully mastered, seems to be supported in part by the young child's new-found capacity to "instruct himself," literally to talk to himself through a sustained sequence. And in part the steadying force seems to be the momentum of concrete overt acts that have a way of sustaining the attention required for their completion by shutting off irrelevant impressions. In time, and with the development of habitual activities, and of language, there emerges more self-directed attention, sometimes called derived primary attention. The child is held steady not so much by vividness as by the habitual round of activity that now demands his attention. Little enough is known about how to help a child become master of his own attention, to sustain it over a long, connected sequence. But while young children are notoriously wandering in their attention, they can be kept in a state of rapt and prolonged attentiveness by being told compelling stories. There may be something to be learned from this observation. What makes the internal sequence of a story even more compelling than the distractions that lie outside it? Are there comparable properties inherent in other activities? Can these be used to train a child to sustain his curiosity beyond the moment's vividness?

Observe a child or group of children building a pile of blocks as high as they can get them. Their attention will be sustained to the flashing point until they reach the climax when the pile comes crashing down. They will return to build still

[1] For a further account of the functions of early curiosity, see J. S. Bruner, "The Cognitive Consequences of Early Sensory Deprivation," *Psychosomatic Medicine*, 21.2:89–95 (1959).

higher. The drama of the task is only its minor virtue. More important is the energizing lure of uncertainty made personal by one's own effort to control it. It is almost the antithesis of the passive attraction of shininess and the vivid. To channel curiosity into more powerful intellectual pursuits requires precisely that there be this transition from the passive, receptive, episodic form of curiosity to the sustained and active form. There are games not only with objects, but with ideas and questions—like Twenty Questions—that provide such a disciplining of the channeling of curiosity. Insofar as one may count on this important human motive—and it seems among the most reliable of the motives—then it seems obvious that our artificial education can in fact be made less artificial from a motivational standpoint by relating it initially to the more surfacy forms of curiosity and attention, and then cultivating curiosity to more subtle and active expression. I think it is fair to say that most of the success in contemporary curriculum building has been achieved by this route. When success comes, it takes the form of recognition that beyond the few things we know there lies a domain of inference: that putting together the two and two that we have yields astonishing results. But this raises the issue of competence, to which we must turn next.

For curiosity is only one of the intrinsic motives for learning. The drive to achieve competence is another. Professor Robert White puts the issue well:

According to Webster, competence means fitness or ability, and the suggested synonyms include capability, capacity, efficiency, proficiency, and skill. It is therefore a suitable word to describe such things as grasping and exploring, crawling and walking, attention and perception, all of which promote an effective—a competent—interaction with the environment. It is true, of course, that maturation plays a part in all these developments, but this part is heavily overshadowed by learning in all the more complex accomplishments like speech or skilled manipulation. I shall argue that it is necessary to make competence a motivational concept; there is *competence motivation* as well as competence in its more familiar sense of achieved capacity. The behavior that leads to the building up of effective grasping, handling, and letting go of objects, to take one example, is not random behavior that is produced by an overflow of energy. It is directed, selective, and persistent, and it continues not because it serves primary drives, which indeed it cannot serve until it is almost perfect, but because it satisfies an intrinsic need to deal with the environment.[2]

Observations of young children and of the young of other species suggest that a good deal of their play must be understood as practice in coping with the environment. Primatologists describe, for example, how young female baboons cradle infant baboons in their arms long before they produce their own offspring. In fact, baboon play can be seen almost entirely as the practice of interpersonal skills. Unlike human children, baboons never play with objects, and this, the anthropologists believe, is connected with their inability to use tools when they grow up. And there is evidence that early language mastery, too, depends on such early preparation. One linguist recently has shown how a two-year-old goes on exploring the limits of language use even after the lights are out, parents removed, communication stopped, and sleep imminent.[3]

The child's metalinguistic play is hard to interpret as anything other than pleasure in practicing and developing a new skill. Although competence may not "naturally" be directed toward school learning, it is certainly possible that the great access of energy that children experience when they "get into a subject they like" is made of the same stuff.

We get interested in what we get good at. In general, it is difficult to sustain interest in an activity unless one achieves some degree of competence. Athletics is the activity par excellence where the young need no prodding to gain pleasure from

[2] R. W. White, "Motivation Reconsidered: The Concept of Competence," *Psychological Review*, 66:297–333 (1959).
[3] Ruth H. Weir, *Language in the Crib* (The Hague: Mouton, 1962).

an increase in skill, save where prematurely adult standards are imposed on little leagues formed too soon to ape the big ones. A custom introduced some years ago at the Gordonstoun School in Scotland has become legendary. In addition to conventionally competitive track and field events within the school, there was established a novel competition in which boys pitted themselves against their own best prior record in the events. Several American schools have picked up the idea and, while there has been no "proper evaluation," it is said that the system creates great excitement and enormous effort on the part of the boys.

To achieve the sense of accomplishment requires a task that has some beginning and some terminus. Perhaps an experiment can serve again as a parable. There is a well-known phenomenon known to psychologists by the forbidding name of the Zeigarnik Effect. In brief, tasks that are interrupted are much more likely to be returned to and completed, and much more likely to be remembered, than comparable tasks that one has completed without interruption. But that puts the matter superficially, for it leaves out of account one factor that is crucial. The effect holds only if the tasks that the subject has been set are ones that have a structure—a beginning, a plan, and a terminus. If the tasks are "silly" in the sense of being meaningless, arbitrary, and without visible means for checking progress, the drive to completion is not stimulated by interruption.

It seems likely that the desire to achieve competence follows the same rule. Unless there is some meaningful unity in what we are doing and some way of telling how we are doing, we are not very likely to strive to excel ourselves. Yet surely this too is only a small part of the story, for everybody does not want to be competent in the same activities, and some competencies might even be a source of embarrassment to their possessors. Boys do not thrill to the challenge of sewing a fine seam (again, in our culture), nor girls to becoming competent

street fighters. There are competencies that are appropriate and
activating for different ages, the two sexes, different social
classes. But there are some things about competence motives
that transcend these particulars. One is that an activity (given
that it is "approved"), must have some meaningful structure
to it if it requires skill that is a little bit beyond that now
possessed by the person—that it be learned by the exercise
of effort. It is probably the combination of the two that is
critical.

Experienced teachers who work with the newer curricula
in science and mathematics report that they are surprised at
the eagerness of students to push ahead to next steps in the
course. Several of the teachers have suggested that the eagerness comes from increased confidence in one's ability to understand the material. Some of the students were having their first
experience of understanding a topic in some depth, of going
somewhere in a subject. It is this that is at the heart of competence motives, and surely our schools have not begun to tap
this enormous reservoir of zest.

While we do not know the limits within which competence
drives can be shaped and channeled by external reward, it
seems quite likely that they are strongly open to external
influence. But channelization aside, how can education keep
alive and nourish a drive to competence—whether expressed
in farming, football, or mathematics? What sustains a sense of
pleasure and achievement in mastering things for their own
sake—what Thorstein Veblen referred to as an instinct for
workmanship? Do competence motives strengthen mainly on
their exercise, in whatever context they may be exercised, or
do they depend also upon being linked to drives for status,
wealth, security, or fame?

There are, to begin with, striking differences among cultures
and between strata within any particular society with respect
to the encouragement given to competence drives. David Mc-

Clelland, for example, in writing about the "achieving society," comments upon the fact that in certain times and places one finds a flowering of achievement motivation strongly supported by the society and its institutions and myths alike.[4] Emphasis upon individual responsibility and initiative, upon dependence in decision and action, upon perfectibility of the self—all of these things serve to perpetuate more basic competency motives past childhood.

But cultures vary in their evaluation of *intellectual* mastery as a vehicle for the expression of competence. Freed Bales, for example, in comparing Irish and Jewish immigrant groups in Boston, remarks that the Jewish, much more than the Irish, treat school success and intellectuality as virtues in their own right as well as ways of upward mobility.[5] The reasons can be found in history. Herzog and Zborowski, in their book on eastern European Jewish communities, suggest that the barrier erected against Jews' entering other professions may have helped foster the cultivation of intellectual excellence as a prized expression of competence.[6]

A culture does not "manage" these matters consciously by the applications of rewards and reproofs alone. The son of the rabbi in the eastern European *stetl* was not punished if he wished to become a merchant rather than a Talmudic scholar, and, indeed, if he chose to become the latter he typically went through long, extrinsically unrewarding, and arduous training to do so. More subtle forces are at work, all of them fairly familiar but too often overlooked in discussing

[4] David C. McClelland, *The Achieving Society* (Princeton, N.J.: Van Nostrand, 1961).

[5] R. Freed Bales, "The 'Fixation Factor' in Alcohol Addiction: A Hypothesis Derived from a Comparative Study of Irish and Jewish Social Norms," unpublished doctoral dissertation, Harvard University, 1944.

[6] Mark Zborowski and Elizabeth Herzog, *Life Is with People: The Jewish Little-Town of Eastern Europe* (New York: International Universities Press, 1952).

education. One of them is "approval." The professional man is more "respected" than the manual worker. But that scarcely exhausts the matter. Respected by whom? Contemporary sociologists speak of the approval of one's "reference group" —those to whom one looks for guides to action, for the definition of the possible, for ultimate approbation. But what leads *this* individual to look to *that* particular reference group?

What appears to be operative is a process we cavalierly call identification. The fact of identification is more easily described than explained. It refers to the strong human tendency to model one's "self" and one's aspirations upon some other person. When we feel we have succeeded in "being like" an identification figure, we derive pleasure from the achievement and, conversely, we suffer when we have "let him down." Insofar as the identification figure is also "a certain kind of person"—belongs to some group or category—we extend our loyalties from an individual to a reference group. In effect, then, identification relates one not only to individuals, but to one's society as well.

While this account is oversimplified, it serves to underline one important feature of identification as a process—its self-sustaining nature. For what it accomplishes is to pass over to the learner the control of punishment and reward. Insofar as we now carry our standards with us, we achieve a certain independence from the immediate rewards and punishments meted out by others.

It has been remarked by psychologists that identification figures are most often those who control the scarce psychological resources that we most desire—love, approval, sustenance. Let me skip this issue for a moment and return to it later.

The term identification is usually reserved for those strong attachments where there is a considerable amount of emotional investment. But there are "milder" forms of identification that are also important during the years of childhood and after. Perhaps we should call those who serve in these milder relationships "competence models." They are the "on the job" heroes, the reliable ones with whom we can interact in some way. Indeed, they control a rare resource, some desired competence, but what is important is that the resource is attainable by interaction. The "on the job" model is nowhere better illustrated than in the manner in which the child learns language from a parent. The tryout-correction-revision process continues until the child comes to learn the rules whereby sentences are generated and transformed appropriately. Finally he develops a set of productive habits that enable him to be his own sentence maker and his own corrector. He "learns the rules of the language." The parent is the model who, by interaction, teaches the skill of language.

In the process of teaching a skill the parent or teacher passes on much more. The teacher imparts attitudes toward a subject and, indeed, attitudes toward learning itself. What results may be quite inadvertent. Often, in our schools, for example, this first lesson is that learning has to do with remembering things when asked, with maintaining a certain undefined tidiness in what one does, with following a train of thought that comes from outside rather than from within and with honoring right answers. Observant anthropologists have suggested that the basic values of the early grades are a stylized version of the feminine role in the society, cautious rather than daring, governed by a ladylike politeness.

One recent study by Pauline Sears underlines the point.[7] It suggests that girls in the early grades, who learn to control their fidgeting earlier and better than boys, are rewarded for excelling in their "feminine" values. The reward can be almost

[7] Pauline Sears, "Attitudinal and Affective Factors Affecting Children's Approaches to Problem Solving," in J. S. Bruner, ed., *Learning about Learning* (Washington, D.C.: U.S. Office of Education, in press).

too successful, so that in later years it is difficult to move girls beyond the orderly virtues they learned in their first school encounters. The boys, more fidgety in the first grade, get no such reward and as a consequence may be freer in their approach to learning in later grades. Far more would have to be known about the other conditions present in the lives of these children to draw a firm conclusion from the findings, but it is nonetheless suggestive. There are surely many ways to expand the range of competence models available to children. One is the use of a challenging master teacher, particularly in the early grades. And there is film or closed-circuit television, opening up enormously the range of teachers to whom the student can be exposed. Filmed teaching has, to be sure, marked limits, for the student cannot interact with an image. But a kind of pseudo interaction can be attained by including in the television lesson a group of students who are being taught right on the screen, with whom the student can take common cause. Team teaching provides still another approach to the exemplification of a range of competences, particularly if one of the teachers is charged specially with the role of gadfly. None of the above is yet a tried practice, but pedagogy, like economics and engineering, often must try techniques to find not only whether they work, but how they may be made to work.

I would like to suggest that what the teacher must be, to be an effective competence model, is a day-to-day working model with whom to interact. It is not so much that the teacher provides a model to *imitate*. Rather, it is that the teacher can become a part of the student's internal dialogue—somebody whose respect he wants, someone whose standards he wishes to make his own. It is like becoming a speaker of a language one shares with somebody. The language of that interaction becomes a part of oneself, and the standards of style and clarity that one adopts for that interaction become a part of one's own standards.

Finally, a word about one last intrinsic motive that bears closely upon the will to learn. Perhaps it should be called reciprocity. For it involves a deep human need to respond to others and to operate jointly with them toward an objective. One of the important insights of modern zoology is the importance of this intraspecies reciprocity for the survival of individual members of the species. The psychologist Roger Barker[8] has commented that the best way he has found to predict the behavior of the children whom he has been studying in great detail in the midst of their everyday activities is to know their situations. A child in a baseball game behaves baseball; in the drugstore the same child behaves drugstore. Situations have a demand value that appears to have very little to do with the motives that are operative. Surely it is not simply a "motive to conform"; this is too great an abstraction. The man who is regulating his pressure on the back of a car, along with three or four others, trying to "rock it out," is not so much conforming as "fitting his efforts into an enterprise." It is about as primitive an aspect of human behavior as we know.

Like the other activities we have been discussing, its exercise seems to be its sole reward. Probably it is the basis of human society, this response through reciprocity to other members of one's species. Where joint action is needed, where reciprocity is required for the group to attain an objective, then there seem to be processes that carry the individual along into learning, sweep him into a competence that is required in the setting of the group. We know precious little about this primitive motive to reciprocate, but what we do know is that it can furnish a driving force to learn as well. Human beings (and other species as well) fall into a pattern that is required by the goals and activities of the social group in which they find themselves. "Imitation" is not the word for it, since it is usually not plain in most cases what is to be imitated. A much more

[8] Roger Barker, "On the Nature of the Environment," *Journal of Social Issues,* 19.4:17–38 (1963).

interesting way of looking at what is involved is provided by the phenomenon of a young child learning to use the pronouns "I" and "you" correctly. The parent says to the child, "You go to bed now." The child says, "No, you no go to bed." We are amused. "Not *me* but *you*," we say. In time, and after a surprisingly brief period of confusion, the child learns that "you" refers to himself when another uses it, and to another person when he uses it—and the reverse with "I." It is a prime example of reciprocal learning. It is by much the same process that children learn the beautifully complicated games they play (adult and child games alike), that they learn their role in the family and in school, and finally that they come to take their role in the greater society.

The corpus of learning, using the word now as synonymous with knowledge, is reciprocal. A culture in its very nature is a set of values, skills, and ways of life that no one member of the society masters. Knowledge in this sense is like a rope, each strand of which extends no more than a few inches along its length, all being intertwined to give a solidity to the whole. The conduct of our educational system has been curiously blind to this interdependent nature of knowledge. We have "teachers" and "pupils," "experts" and "laymen." But the community of learning is somehow overlooked.

What can most certainly be encouraged—and what is now being developed in the better high schools—is something approximating the give and take of a seminar in which discussion is the vehicle of instruction. This is reciprocity. But it requires recognition of one critically important matter: you cannot have both reciprocity and the demand that everybody learn the same thing or be "completely" well rounded in the same way all the time. If reciprocally operative groups are to give support to learning by stimulating each person to join his efforts to a group, then we shall need tolerance for the specialized roles that develop—the critic, the innovator, the second helper, the cautionary. For it is from the cultivation of these interlocking roles that the participants get the sense of operating reciprocally in a group. Never mind that this pupil for this term in this seminar has a rather specialized task to perform. It will change. Meanwhile, if he can see how he contributes to the effectiveness of the group's operations on history or geometry or whatnot, he is likely to be the more activated. And surely one of the roles that will emerge is that of auxiliary teacher—let it, encourage it. It can only help in relieving the tedium of a classroom with one expert up here and the rest down there.

At the risk of being repetitious, let me restate the argument. It is this. The will to learn is an intrinsic motive, one that finds both its source and its reward in its own exercise. The will to learn becomes a "problem" only under specialized circumstances like those of a school, where a curriculum is set, students confined, and a path fixed. The problem exists not so much in learning itself, but in the fact that what the school imposes often fails to enlist the natural energies that sustain spontaneous learning—curiosity, a desire for competence, aspiration to emulate a model, and a deep-sensed commitment to the web of social reciprocity. Our concern has been with how these energies may be cultivated in support of school learning. If we know little firmly, at least we are not without reasonable hypotheses about how to proceed. The practice of education does, at least, produce interesting hypotheses. After all, the Great Age of Discovery was made possible by men whose hypotheses were formed before they had developed a decent technique for measuring longitude.

You will have noted by now a considerable de-emphasis of "extrinsic" rewards and punishments as factors in school learning. There has been in these pages a rather intentional neglect of the so-called Law of Effect, which holds that a reaction is more likely to be repeated if it has previously been followed by a "satisfying state of affairs." I am not unmindful of the notion of reinforcement. It is doubtful, only, that "satisfying states of affairs" are *reliably* to be found outside learning itself—in kind or harsh words from the teacher, in grades and gold stars, in the absurdly abstract assurance to the high school student that his lifetime earnings will be better by 80 percent if he graduates. External reinforcement may indeed get a particular act going and may even lead to its repetition, but it does not nourish, reliably, the long course of learning by which man slowly builds in his own way a serviceable model of what the world is and what it can be.

Chapter **7**

On Coping
and Defending

WE PSYCHOLOGISTS have developed a curious posture. It can best be summed up by the apologetic note we strike when we speak of normality. Indeed, my colleagues more often than not insert a quote in their tone of voice or inscribe inverted commas in the air when referring to "normal" controls or to "normal" states, and at a scientific meeting I recently attended a member of the audience addressed a question to the speaker about his "so-called normal group." Yet this wariness about normality is not all a posture. It is in part a compassionate recognition of man's vulnerability to trouble, an awareness that being sick and being well are matters of subtle balance. But a vice is often fashioned from an excess of virtue, and so our attitude about the feather line between health and illness may lead us to overlook some of the important differences between them.

I should like to consider one of the differences between psychological health and illness—the distinction between coping and defending. And I should like to limit the matter further by concentrating upon the reflection these cast on a human being's intellectual life. Coping respects the requirements of problems we encounter while still respecting our integrity. Defending is a strategy whose objective is avoiding or escaping from problems for which we believe there is no solution that does not violate our integrity of functioning.

Integrity of functioning is some required level of self-con-
sistency or style, a need to solve problems in a manner consistent with our most valued life enterprises. Given the human
condition, neither coping nor defending is found often in pure
form. The imperiousness of our drives and the demands of
powerful, nonrational, and indocile unconscious mechanisms
force some measure of defense. And, save in the deteriorated
psychotic, it is rare for defense to cut a person off entirely
from the requirements of daily living. Even the most extreme
schizophrenic can usually cope with severe emergency—indeed, shock therapy may depend for what effectiveness it has
upon the arousal of such coping.

   Yet, notwithstanding that there is always a mixture of
coping and defending in dealing with life as we find it, I
would urge that we distinguish sharply between the two processes. Let me recount what has led me to this conclusion. It
begins with a serious error of oversimplification in the design
of a research project in which several of my colleagues and
I were engaged. Our interest was in studying learning effectiveness. We took it as axiomatic that the object of any particular piece of learning was not only to master the task before
one, but to master it in such a way that one would be saved
from subsequent learning of identical or like tasks. This
seemed to us self-evident and still seems so, for unless learning
were rendered generic the organism would be constantly
locked in trial and error that would leave him in perpetual
danger, and this does not seem to be how organisms act. The
question we were asking was, how do organisms benefit from
past experience so that future experience can be handled with
minimum pain and effort? This constitutes learning effectiveness, of which the problem of transfer is one part. The design
of our project was quite conventional. We would study a group
of normal children (in quotes, of course) and compare their
approach to learning with that of a group of children referred

to a guidance clinic for "learning blocks"—children of normal or superior intelligence, without other evident behavior disorders, who were unable to learn in school. Preliminary observation of such children had led us too simply to the conclusion that it was not so much that they had grave difficulties in learning as that they seemingly learned in such a way that there was little or no transfer to new situations, in consequence of which they were constantly having to learn *de novo*. There is a little truth to this observation, but it is quite trivial. It was our hope to design a set of testing and observational procedures that would indicate quantitatively the manner in which the group who were effective differed from the other group who were not.

Fortunately for us, we began our inquiry with a clinical and therapeutic study of some half-dozen children referred to the Judge Baker Guidance Center for "learning blocks." The children were in therapy, and were also tutored in their schoolwork by us with the dual aim of helping them and discovering at close range how they went about learning. The parents of the children were also seeing psychiatric social workers regularly. Withal, we had an opportunity for quite close observation. It became apparent after some months of work that the learning activities of our disturbed children had certain distinctive features that had very little directly to do with the nature of effectiveness—save in the sense that the processes we observed interfered with effectiveness. In a word, their efforts to defend themselves from the activity of learning and from its consequences made it extremely difficult for them to get to the activity of "school learning" itself. Their schoolwork created certain psychological problems that were much more compelling than school problems and that drastically altered their approach to conventional school learning. They could not, in short, cope with the demands of schoolwork unless and until they were able to defend themselves against the panic of impulse and anxiety that the demands of schoolwork set off in them. Here, then, was a classic antinomy. It was not that they were unable to learn in the conventional sense of that word— for in fact there was much learned canniness in their defensiveness against learning, and later there was often much talent in the way in which they approached school problems when the clamor of defense requirements had been in part quieted.

One will say, "But the difference between these children and the children who do well in school is not in *how* they are learning but in *what* they are learning—the one group geometry and the other, say, how to handle hostility toward their teacher." But this again appears not to be the case. The very texture of the learning in the two instances appears different. Consider the matter more systematically.

Recall first our earlier description of the learning process as it develops in children. At its beginnings, it is shot through with action. It is not surprising that children often hold the belief that thinking something and doing it are somehow equivalent. We shall return to this point later. A second feature of early acquisition of knowledge is that ideas are not isolated from their motivational or emotional context. Thus we find children as old as eleven who block at naming any similarity between one object they happen to like and another they are frightened of—say, a cat and a dog—though they are quite capable of grouping together water and milk as things that you drink. The example is an emotionally trivial one, and later we shall encounter more meaningful instances. When early learning is hemmed around with conflict, as it so often is by virtue of being made a road to parental approval and love or a weapon in the arsenal of sibling rivalry, with the consequence that it becomes highly charged or libidinized, the affective links that relate concepts and ideas often are powerful and relatively intractable, in the sense that they persist in fantasy and can be found to intrude in the child's thinking in later school settings.

At the unverbalized level, then, the child approaches the task of school learning, with its highly rationalistic and formal patterns, with a legacy of unconscious logic in which action, affect, and conceptualization are webbed together. Feeling and action and thought can substitute for each other, and there is an equation governed by what in grammar is called synechdoche: feelings can stand for things, actions for things, things for feelings, parts for wholes. It is as evident as it is both fortunate and unfortunate that these early cognitive structures remain in being into adult life—evident in the sense that the structures appear in dream and in free association and, in a disciplined form, in the products of the artist; fortunate in the sense that without such structures there would neither be poets and painters nor an audience for them; unfortunate in the sense that when this mode of functioning is compulsively a feature of a person's life, he is not able to adjust to the requirements of any but a specially arranged environment.

There are several other features of early learning that are less distinctive but nonetheless important. One of them is the inability of the young child to delay gratification once he has completed a task or to set goals that place that gratification in the far future. These shortcomings have very real consequences. One is that learning is in short pieces, with very little by way of a comprehensive, large-scale structure.[1] That is to say, the more logical and hierarchical structures are lacking —genus-species, cause-effect, rule-example. But though the child may not link many events together in this more logical fashion, he relates them through the associations they share in action and affect. These early, more turbulent forms of learning are extrinsically motivated—being controlled and shaped by gratifications outside of learning itself. Many of the affects and gratifications that give structure to earliest experi-

[1] See J. S. Bruner, R. R. Olver, P. M. Greenfield, et al., *Studies in Cognitive Growth* (New York: John Wiley & Sons, 1966).

ence are products of taboo and prohibition encountered in socialization. And so too the ideational connections learned under their sway. They become the "dangerous thoughts" of childhood. Such charged cognitive structures may form the core of what later become the *preemptive metaphors* of defensive cognitive activity—a matter that will occupy us shortly. Intrinsic learning that provides its own reward, less subject to such vicissitudes, represents, in contrast, what might be considered the beginnings of a "conflict-free sphere of the ego," characterized by the curiosity and competence-seeking discussed in the essay "The Will to Learn."

Let me suggest now that effective cognitive learning in school depends upon a denaturing process, if I may use such a fanciful and abrasive expression. It involves at least three things. There must first develop a system of cognitive organization that detaches concepts from the modes of action that they evoke. A hole is to dig, but it is also a hole. Secondly, it requires the development of a capacity to detach concepts from their affective contexts. A hole is not just a reminder of a hidden orifice. Finally, it demands a capacity to delay gratification so that the outcomes of acts can be treated as information rather than as simply punishing or rewarding.

The denaturing process of which I speak probably depends upon the presence of several conditions in the early history of the child. Let me abbreviate them to *stimulation, play, identification,* and some degree of *freedom from drive and anxiety.* With respect to stimulation, what is crucial is that the child have an opportunity to grow beyond enactive representation with its action-bound immediacy and beyond iconic representation with its strong susceptibility to affective linkage, described in the first essay. Varied stimulation with relative freedom from stress is about the only way we know of promoting such growth.

With respect to play and playfulness, it is first of all an attitude in which the child learns that the outcomes of various activities are not as extreme as he either hoped or feared—it involves learning to place limits on the anticipated consequences of activity. We have been struck by the difference in parents in respect to their encouragement of playfulness in their children—the children whose learning blocks we have studied and normal schoolchildren. In some instances, among normal children, we are told of "breast play" in which the very consequential act of nursing at the breast is altered into an occasion for playing—nipple in and out in a kind of loving tease. And throughout growth, it is as in the famous remark of Niels Bohr to one of his graduate students who complained of the seeming unseriousness, the amount of horseplay and joking, around Bohr's laboratory: "But there are some things so important that one can only joke about them." In time, the attitude of play is converted into what may best be called a game attitude in which the child gets the sense not only that consequences are limited but that the limitation comes by virtue of a set of rules that govern a procedure, whether it be checkers or arithmetic or baseball. It was a standard line of nineteenth-century evolutionary thinking that the function of play was to permit the organism to try out his repertory of response in preparation for the later, serious business of surviving against the pressures of his habitat. It can be argued equally well that, for human beings at least, play serves the function of reducing the pressures of impulse and incentive and making it possible thereby for intrinsic learning to begin; for if ever there is self-reward in process it is in the sphere of "doing things for merriment," particularly things that might otherwise be too serious in Niels Bohr's sense.

As for identification, recall that willingness to learn, particularly in middle-class families, and particularly among boys, is a prime way of expressing identification with family ideals. One way in which learning becomes highly charged with conflict is through conflict with a family competence model who stands for, and gives rewards for, learning. There are many ways in which identification conflicts arise, but the consequence of most of them is that the child ends up with a rejected competence ideal and no adequate pattern to guide his growth. Whether, in the case of a boy, he is the victim of a father who systematically and sarcastically attacks his son's efforts at mastery, or of one who, as a staff therapist put it, "tip-toes his way through life," the result is that the child fails to develop the sense that he can prevail by his own efforts.

Finally, the matter of freedom from excessive drive. There is good evidence that too strong an incentive for learning narrows the learning and renders it less generic, in the sense of its being less transferable. Where learning is dominated by strong extrinsic rewards and punishments, it becomes specific to the requirements of the particular learning task. It is almost a universal observation of parents that there comes a time of pressure in almost any child's school career when the child blocks, becomes "functionally stupid." A constant pressure of this kind not only produces the narrowing and the transitory block, but may have the effect of keeping active some of the primitive processes of early learning described before—or even leading a child to regress to these more primitive processes to such an extent that action, affect, and thought are fused in a preemptive metaphor, a matter to which we now turn.

What is a preemptive metaphor and what conditions seem to favor its dominance? It represents a principle of cognitive organization that is complexive rather than conceptual.[2] The organization centers upon an affective concept like "things that can hurt me," within which any potentially disruptive or hurtful thing can then be included. For the acceptance criterion of such a concept is the loose rule of synecdoche by which parts

---

[2] See L. S. Vygotsky, *Thought and Language,* ed. and trans. by Eugenia Hanfmann and Gertrude Vakar (New York: John Wiley & Sons, 1962), and especially the account of Rose R. Olver's work in Bruner, Olver, Greenfield et al., *Studies in Cognitive Growth.*

can stand for wholes. Let me illustrate by reference to two examples from our case records. In one instance we are dealing with a fourteen-year-old with a severe learning block, a boy with an estimated IQ of 125 whose failing grades are far below what one would expect from one of such intelligence. And indeed, on rare occasions he will show his colors by a sharp improvement in his work, but it is then followed by regression. The mother is the dominant figure in the family, and when she and her husband were high school students before marriage, she helped him through his studies. The boy's sister, the "learner" in the family, is now in the same position with respect to this boy. For the boy, learning is to a certain degree an act of feminization, in part an act of rejection and hostility toward the father. On the rare occasions when he has shown improvement in his school studies, he has gone out of his way to injure himself by exposing himself to danger—by climbing on roofs, by taking foolish chances skiing, and so forth. The injuries are a retribution for the aggressive act of learning—an act he sees directed against his father.

Angus Strong, to use his clinical name, shows a preoccupation with injury and bodily harm.[3] The range of objects and events that can cause harm, as he acts out his fantasies, is very great and comprises many aspects of his schoolwork. He dislikes fractions, for example, and cannot work readily with them, for he sees them as "cut-up numbers." The elementary operation of cancelation in algebra symbolizes for him the act of "killing off numbers and letters on each side of the equal sign." Asked to extrapolate from three ascending points on a graph, he draws a line through and slightly beyond the points and then has it descend in a sharp drop: "It can get up

[3] For a full clinical account, see M. A. Wallach, D. N. Ulrich, and Margaret B. Grunebaum, "The Relationship of Family Disturbance to Cognitive Difficulties in a Learning-Problem Child," *Journal of Consulting Psychology,* 24:355–360 (1960).

that far, and then it's sure to explode and fall again." Or he says, "Watch out for that pencil; it has a sharp point," and then later, "That piece of wood is dangerous because you can sharpen its end and it can hurt you."

What Angus appears to be doing is scanning his environment for anything that can be related to his central retribution-and-injury theme. Once he finds it, he then incorporates it into a kind of fantasy about how to avoid hurt or how to bring the harm under his own control rather than being caught out by it. The organization of the concept "what-will-hurt-me" has a seemingly chaotic quality, but only seemingly so. One soon realizes that it is based on a limitless metaphor whose function is to guarantee that Angus will not "miss anything that might hurt me or lead me to hurt those toward whom I feel hostile." It is this type of almost cancerous growth of a preempting metaphor that is the basis of the kind of learning that supports defense and makes coping virtually impossible. For so long as organization is dominated by so exigent an internal requirement—not missing anything dangerous lest one be overwhelmed by it—it is difficult to gain the detachment necessary to treat new materials and tasks in their own terms, free of the compellingly preemptive context to which they have been assigned.

Let me contrast this sample of Angus's behavior with the reactions of a group of twelve-year-old children in seventh-grade arithmetic class—children whom we had observed systematically for three years. Asked what they had liked best in arithmetic up to that year, the majority's response was "fractions." As one child put it, "There are so many things you can do with fractions." So while Angus was locked in the metaphoric significance of fractions as being "cut up," his age-mates were gaining a sense of mastery and manipulation based on such delightful insights as the equivalence of $\frac{1}{2}$, $\frac{2}{4}$, $\frac{3}{6}$, and $n/2n$. But it is not simply this, either, for there are striking differences in how the normal, coping children were going about fractions—their willingness to recognize the generality of the series just mentioned and their practice with such generalities.

There seem to be at least two ways in which preemptive metaphors operate in the blocked child. One is best described as "assimilation." Once an object or event is identified as related to the defensive preemptive metaphor, it is assimilated to the fantasies and "actings out" that are also related to the metaphor. The new object or event is then reacted to in old, established neurotic ways. A second way in which the preemptive metaphor operates is by denial. Once an event is "matched" to the preemptive metaphor, it is then avoided, pushed out of mind, "overignored." Let me illustrate the latter pattern by reference to the case of Dick Kleinman, one of our young patients, in treatment from age twelve to fifteen.

Dick's family was dominated during his early years by a father who relieved his sense of inadequacy by depreciating and punishing Dick for failure to live up to standards far in excess of what could reasonably be expected of the boy— neatness in eating, reasoning ability, and so on. The father suffered a chronic heart condition, but Dick was not told about it because his parents were afraid the information might get back to the father's employer. All Dick knew was that he was not to make noise when his father was about, not to disturb him, and, above all, not to make him angry. Dick was born after the other children in the family were grown. He was an "accident," and his mother rather resented him while getting real gratification from his dependence upon her, a dependence she cultivated. There were episodes during Dick's early childhood of sudden separation from the mother—she went off to the hospital, and another time he was sent off to relatives when she underwent orthopedic surgery. Two considerably older sisters, each of whom had served Dick in the role of mother, departed for marriage during his early childhood. His work in school was indifferent from the start and his teachers complained of inattention. By the time he reached eleven, it was apparent that he was falling further and further behind. He made few friends and was usually in a subdued and depressive mood. As he approached twelve, he began therapy. Shortly afterwards his father died of a heart attack, Dick having no forewarning.

For Dick, inquiry or active curiosity, in contrast to passive acceptance, had led to punishment or to scorn as aggressive and noisy. His attempts at "figuring things out" had been often enough and sarcastically dismissed by his father. The depreciating attitude of the father was reinforced by the mother, who treated Dick as incompetent to do schoolwork. She said to me when we first met after I had become Dick's tutor, "Do you think you can *really* do anything with him?" In his family, Dick had models neither of playfulness nor competence, and nobody who could help him develop a free and flexible attitude to learning. Indeed, the family attitude toward knowing things was even flawed by a curious "pushing aside" of the unpalatable as unmentionable. This creation of a sphere of unmentionable and unthinkable things—father's illness, mother's health problems, the marriage of a cousin to a Chinese, and so on—took with Dick. He seemed a most uncurious boy.

His approach to learning seemed to lack any aim at mastery. He sought instead to register what was told him or what was read, and made little effort to organize or go beyond. Some examples will give the flavor. His biology class was given the topic of photosynthesis; a tutorial session was scheduled that afternoon. I asked Dick what photosynthesis was. His account was garbled; its one virtue was that he had obviously committed to rote memory the principal words and phrases the teacher had used in describing the process. I asked him whether he felt he understood it, and he replied tentatively in the affirmative. I then said to him that I would tell him my version of it and we'd see whether they matched, and proceeded to set forth an even more garbled account, again using Dick's key phrases. When I was done, he nodded and said that was how he understood it, too, and he then tried to go on to the next topic. The remainder of the hour was given over to giving him a simple picture of photosynthesis that he could really understand, and doing it in a way that would assure him that the effort to understand would not be greeted by scorn or sarcasm. He reacted in a manner that was to become typical—elaborating and going back over the material he had now dared to understand, very much depending upon the tutor's support as he dared try out his mastery. A session on "sentence craft," as it is called, provides a second example. Poorly constructed sentences were to be rewritten so that they would be less ambiguous and more compact. Dick's efforts were of little avail: his rearranged sentences were no better and often even more opaque than those in the exercise book. Again, the same procedure, giving him simple examples so that he would not panic. In time, he got the idea; he would read the original aloud and then his revision, to hear whether the second "made more sense" than the first. A lucky image emerged during the course of all this. When he succeeded for the first time on a simply garbled sentence, I made as if to turn a switch on his forehead, "You see, it is like turning a switch in your head, then you do it the way you just did." He responded with laughing agreement. Some days later he said, "But how will I know I have a sentence right when I do them at home?" I suggested he phone me each morning during the coming week just before leaving for school, and said that I would listen to but not correct his work. For a week he was my guaranteed alarm clock. By the day before our next weekly tutorial, we went through our telephone ritual almost as a joke. He had mastered the task with lots to spare.

In Dick's case, as I have indicated, it was the activity of learning and mental inquiry that had been captured by a pre-

emptive metaphor, the activity of thinking about unknowns
and new eventualities. Such activity had led either to dangerous
consequences or to punishment. The metaphoric structure that
guided his defensive activity included learning, questioning,
curiosity, inquisitiveness. Learning tested his mother's right to
dominate, renewed his hostile fears of his father, spelled the
possibility of failure and loss. The solution was to keep it
suppressed, under wraps. What his tutor did was to make it
easy for him to discover that learning was neither very dangerous nor likely to evoke punitive and sarcastic response.
Unlike Angus, Dick did not assimilate dangerous activity into
a fantasy context. Rather, his pattern was one of avoidance
and denial—finding techniques of rote learning that would,
in effect, keep the dangerous activity from entering the structure of his thinking.

But the assimilative and the avoidant activities overdefend
in a costly way. Each requires a constant scanning of the
environment for whatever might be relevant to the core conflict that is the source of trouble. The result is a highly distract-
ing preoccupation: children with this kind of difficulty miss
out on a good deal of what is going on because they have such
an absorbing investment in scanning the world for danger. It
is not surprising, then, that teachers often report that these
children are inattentive or that they never participate in class
discussions. Our children in treatment often missed what the
next day's assignment was—either literally or in the sense of
not grasping its purpose—and it has occurred to us that perhaps the time of maximal upset and defense comes just as they
are getting into new material and unknown situations, as at
the moment of a new assignment.

But there is one other factor operating in the distraction
of these children. It has in considerable measure to do with
the nature of the conflict that underlies their difficulties. Consider now the origin of learning blocks.

The child with a learning block is the classic case of the

double bind—he is damned if he succeeds and damned if he fails. If he fails in his schoolwork, he suffers at school and at home; if he succeeds, he suffers at home and alone. Let me give some typical examples. One child has a younger sister who is mongoloid, a fact the family have had great difficulty admitting to themselves. Their attention is focused on the uncertain progress of younger sister, and great pressure is placed on the twelve-year-old boy to take care of himself and be on his own. In his view, succeeding at school (and his IQ is adequate for that) means less attention from his parents. Indeed, his mother said to the social worker, "If Tony gets along well in school, then that means we don't have to worry about him. We have plenty to worry about already." So success means the loss of a cherished dependency relationship. If, on the other hand, he gets failing grades in school, he is treated harshly at home for his failure, but in any case he gets some of the family's attention. Both success and failure are, then, fraught with difficulties. In the case of another boy, learning is an instrument for controlling and striking back at his parents, though the child is unaware of it, and there is naturally a good deal of anxiety attached to school performance. When he is faced with the idea of growing up, he stands to lose even this much control over his parents. Or, in the case of Dick, the dangers of learning are balanced by praise at home, but also by a sense of his mother's demand that he continue to be her baby. Avoidance of learning satisfies defensive demands, but it too leads to trouble. Finally, with Angus, his failure at school is almost a precondition for peace in the family situation, a condition for his self-identification as a man, where men are assumed to be the ones not good at school and women help them. It is not surprising that learning becomes so consequential for these children that a playful attitude and perspective cannot develop normally.

Yet what must seem patent—and particularly so to those who have children of school age—is that, in some measure, the double bind is the plight of every child growing up in our society. Perhaps there are two or three things that make the difference in the children who become the victims of it. The first is sheer intensity. So tight is the bind in these children that a drastic defensive expedient finally emerges. I am inclined to believe that the second major factor is the absence of an adequate competence figure for the child to identify with. All our cases were boys, and most cases referred to clinics are. The ineffective fathers and the ones who express an impotent rage provide no workable model for mastery, as Barbara Kimball showed a decade ago. And so, too, the overpowering, rejecting fathers who demand so much that only opposition remains as an alternative. Identification seems to provide the modeling or patterning that leads the child toward coping rather than defending. But neither the intensity of the double bind nor the unavailability of a competence model for identification appears sufficient explanation. All of the children we have seen show a tell-tale lack of awareness of what they are doing—whether the pattern is one of assimilation or of avoidance. The learning block is not an instance of rebellion and overt refusal to study or attend to lessons. The children observed fail in their work even when they try—and in some cases (as with Dick) trying was the worst prescription. Whatever "the unconscious" means, these children were operating by its direction. In effect, it amounts, I suppose, to a set of cognitive operations that prevail in the absence of conscious controls. The preemptive quality of the defensive metaphor seems to be the hallmark of such unawareness. To be sure, much ordinary thinking is metaphoric, and surely Wittgenstein has taught us in our generation not to use strict rules of categorization as criteria for judging daily thinking. But it is the absence of the conscious or "logical" check that permits a defensive metaphor to grow by a cancerous metastasis. In the absence of such checks, it is virtually impossible to "denature" or "delibidinize" learning. In severe cases, defense becomes so

nd a close reading of Freud certainly indicates that h
 believe so. The "primary process" of infantile thinkin
ely not for Freud the basis of later, more world-oriented
dary process."

 word, then, coping and defending are not, in my
, processes of the same kind that differ merely in degree.
iffer in kind. What poses the eternal challenge to the
 is the knowledge that the metaphoric processes can,
ut under the constraints of conscious problem solving,
he interests of healthy functioning. Without those con-
, they result in the crippling decline that comes from a
ization on defense.

habitual that it is almost impossible to make quick therapeutic progress in substituting coping for defending where school learning is concerned.

Consider now the nature of therapy. To what extent does therapeutic progress reflect the kind of processes I have been describing? Let me say at the outset that I lay no claim to wide clinical experience with children. Yet I must at least put down the observations we have made and let those with more experience judge their pertinence to the general problems of therapy with children. It has seemed to us in the first place that therapy with our group of children required considerably more than an intrapsychic working through of unconscious material. Working through, yes, particularly if some insight was to be achieved and the constraints of awareness assisted in containing the defensive activity we have described as the preemptive metaphor. But the tutorial was also a crucial factor in helping the child learn to cope. It mattered first in enabling the child to establish a learning situation free of the double bind. Take the eleven-year-old boy who at one of his first sessions said to the tutor that he was afraid to make an error in reading because his teacher yelled at him. The tutor asked whether his teacher yelled very loud, and, upon being assured that she did, volunteered that he could yell louder than the teacher, and urged his patient to make a mistake and see. The boy did, and his tutor in mock voice yelled as loud as he could. The boy jumped. Tutor to patient: "Can she yell louder than that?" Patient: "Yes, lots." Tutor: "Make another error and I'll try to get louder still." The game went on three or four rounds, and the tutor then suggested that the patient try yelling when he, the tutor, made an error. (The tutor was Dr. Michael Maccoby.) After a few sessions, a playful relation had been built up about mistakes in reading, and the beginnings of transference were at hand. Soon the child was able to take satisfaction in the skills in which he was achieving mastery.

The episodes of "sentence craft" and Dick's reaction to them are similarly relevant. Supporting a dependency relationship up to a point—that point being where Dick had to do the actual work of sentence revision himself and judge whether his own performance was correct, the tutor providing the emotional support—had the effect of getting Dick across the line into intrinsic learning. There were comparable episodes in his algebra, where the idea of unknowns to be solved troubled him. Once that was turned into something of a game we played between us, his grasp of the ways of algebra grew on its own. Biology was the next area, and again tutorial therapy ran from initial emotional support to self-propulsion. To be sure, progress was being made at the same time in dealing both with Dick's family situation and with his own intrapsychic conflicts. Yet what was most observable was the manner in which, once tension was reduced, either by means of conventional therapy or the implicit therapy of a supporting tutorial relationship, the child himself would begin to take over and get a sense of reward from such competence as he had managed to establish. If the supporting relationship remained intact, the competence would be extended and the kind of coping necessary to a task would begin in earnest. The tutor as identification figure became increasingly important in all this, for the tutor provided a new model of coping by showing that problems are both soluble and not dangerous —or, when not soluble, at least not the source of either disaster or punishment.

In the end, then, we too were impressed by the sharpness of the difference between coping and defending. When the child could meet the requirements of the tasks set him, the spreading pattern of defense would fade. There was little in common between the two approaches.

What may we conclude about coping and defending?

What seems clearest to me is that there is a deep discon-

tinuity between the two not only in th[e] the nature of the processes involved. the need for locating whatever may b its reasonable goal by including in its be construed as dangerous. Unconstr[ained] cesses, defense operates by the use o[f] emptive metaphor—literally a kind of under extreme stress, finally implicates world as being potentially dangerous This is the mode of the unconscious, s unlikely that, on its own, "the uncons[cious] a creative source of thinking. Rather when the metaphoric processes come in some degree that they can serve a with problems—what in recent years sion in the service of the ego."

What seems to be required for a p for the requirements of problem sol intellectual activity from the deman[ds] affect, and drive. We have suggeste[d] depends upon a child's having the playfulness to develop, upon his havi[ng] tence model available, and upon the reward from increased competence th "learning for its own sake." These p[r]

There is a form of pedagogical ro[mance] arousal of unconscious, creative impul to learning. One would do well to doctrine. As Lawrence Kubie and unconscious impulses unconstrained b sense of play can be quite the contr[a] often taken for granted that the proce[sses] cognitive functioning are mere ext dream work and association. I do n[ot]

case, a did no was su "secon

In a opinio They teache when serve t straint special

A Retrospect on Making and Judging

IN THE foregoing essays, I have tried to explore the relation between two enterprises, each difficult enough on its own. One is the course of intellectual development, the other pedagogy. In the introductory essay, I sketched how I had become involved in such a joint undertaking. A decade ago, when I first became engaged in this work, it seemed obvious enough to me, as to others, that the two domains must be related, and it was my hope that, betimes, the relation would become clear to me. Indeed, the various essays in this book were attempts to bring some order to the vexed problem of the relation between pedagogy and intellectual development, how the one might assist the other.

What must be plain in the preceding chapters is that the issues to be faced are far broader than those conventionally comprised in what is called "education" or "child rearing." Our proper subject is, of course, how a culture is transmitted —its skills, values, style, technology, and wisdom—and how, in transmission, it produces more effective and zestful human beings. Can we gain some perspective on the matter by examining the evolution of such transmission?

It is, of course, impossible to reconstruct the evolution in techniques of instruction in the shadow zone between early hominids and present man. I have tried to compensate by observing contemporary analogues of earlier forms, knowing

full well that the pursuit of analogy can be dangerously misleading. I have spent many hours observing uncut films of the
behavior of free-ranging baboons, films shot in East Africa by
my colleague Professor Irven DeVore with a very generous
footage devoted to infants and juveniles. I have also had access
to the unedited film archives of a hunting-gathering people
living under roughly analogous ecological conditions, the
!Kung Bushman of the Kalahari, recorded by Laurance and
Lorna Marshall, brilliantly aided by their son John and daughter Elizabeth. I have also worked directly but informally with
the Wolof of Senegal, observing children in the bush and in
French-style schools. Even more valuable than my own informal observations in Senegal were the systematic experiments
carried out later by my colleague, Patricia Marks Greenfield.[1]

Let me describe very briefly some salient differences in the
free learning patterns of immature baboons and among !Kung
children. Baboons have a highly developed social life in their
troops, with well-organized and stable dominance patterns.
They live within a territory, protecting themselves from predators by joint action of the strongly built, adult males. It is
striking that the behavior of baboon juveniles is shaped principally by play with their peer group, play that provides
opportunity for the spontaneous expression and practice of
the component acts that, in maturity, will be orchestrated into
the behavior either of the dominant male or of the infant-
protective female. All this seems to be accomplished with little
participation by any mature animals in the play of the juveniles. We know from the important experiments of Harlow and
his colleagues how devastating a disruption in development can
be produced in sub-human primates by interfering with their
opportunity for peer-group play and social interaction.[2]

Among hunting-gathering humans, on the other hand, there

[1] See Dr. Greenfield's chapters in Bruner, Olver, Greenfield et al.,
Studies in Cognitive Growth (New York: John Wiley & Sons, 1966).

[2] H. Harlow and Margaret Harlow, "Social Deprivation in Monkeys,"
Scientific American, November 1962.

is *constant* interaction between adult and child, adult and adolescent, adolescent and child. !Kung adults and children play and dance together, sit together, participate in minor hunting together, join in song and storytelling together. At very frequent intervals, moreover, children are party to rituals presided over by adults—minor, as in the first haircutting, or major, as when a boy kills his first kudu buck and goes through the proud but painful process of scarification. Children, besides, are constantly playing imitatively with the rituals, implements, tools, and weapons of the adult world. Young juvenile baboons, on the other hand, almost never play with things or imitate directly large and significant sequences of adult behavior.

Note, though, that in tens of thousands of feet of !Kung film, one virtually never sees an instance of "teaching" taking place outside the situation where the behavior to be learned is relevant. Nobody teaches in our prepared sense of the word. There is nothing like school, nothing like lessons. Indeed, among the !Kung there is very little "telling." Most of what we would call instruction is through showing. And there is no practice or drill as such save in the form of play modeled directly on adult models—play hunting, play bossing, play exchanging, play baby tending, play house making. In the end, every man in the culture knows nearly all there is to know about how to get on with life as a man, and every woman as a woman—the skills, the rituals and myths, the obligations and rights.

The change in the instruction of children in more complex societies is twofold. First of all, there is knowledge and skill in the culture far in excess of what any one individual knows. And so, increasingly, there develops an economical technique of instructing the young based heavily on *telling* out of context rather than *showing* in context. In literate societies, the practice becomes institutionalized in the school or the teacher. Both promote this necessarily abstract way of instructing the young.

The result of "teaching the culture" can, at its worst, lead to the ritual, rote nonsense that has led a generation of critics to despair. For, in the detached school, what is imparted often has little to do with life as lived in the society except in so far as the demands of school are of a kind that reflect *indirectly* the demands of life in a technical society. But these indirectly imposed demands may be the most important feature of the detached school. For school is a sharp departure from indigenous practice. It takes learning, as we have noted, out of the context of immediate action just by dint of putting it into a school. This very disengagement makes learning become an act in itself, freed from the immediate ends of action, preparing the learner for the chain of reckoning remote from payoff that is needed for the formulation of complex ideas. At the same time, the school (if successful) frees the child from the pace setting of the round of daily activity. If the school succeeds in avoiding a pace-setting round of its own, it may be one of the great agents for promoting reflectiveness. Moreover, in school, one must "follow the lesson," which means one must learn to follow either the abstraction of written speech—abstract in the sense that it is divorced from the concrete situation to which the speech might originally have been related—or the abstraction of language delivered orally but out of the context of an on-going action. Both of these are highly abstract uses of language.

It is no wonder, then, that many recent studies report large differences between "primitive" children who are in schools and their brothers who are not: differences in perception, abstraction, time perspective, and so on. I need only cite the work of Biesheuvel in South Africa,[3] Gay and Cole in Liberia,[4]

[3] S. Biesheuvel, "Psychological Tests and Their Application to Non-European Peoples," in *The Yearbook of Education* (London: Evans Brothers, 1949), pp. 87–126.

[4] J. Gay and M. Cole, "Outline of General Report on Kpelle Mathematics Project," mimeographed, n.d.

Greenfield in Senegal, Maccoby and Modiano in rural Mexico, Reich among Alaskan Eskimos.[5]

I shall not pause here to consider what is involved in the first two ways of becoming a grown organism—either growing up baboon or growing up in an indigenous society. The latter has had its share of attention in the literature on culture and personality. Even so, there has been little enough effort expended in trying to understand in some decently detailed way how a young man, say, learns not only to hunt but to recognize the necessary blend of technique and ritual—learns the pattern of sharing as well as of hunting. The Bushman, for example, knows extraordinarily exquisite rules about how meat is to be shared after a hunt—what is his own share, what belongs to the owner of the arrow that was "lent" to him as a gift, what belongs to this kinsman and that, and so forth.[6] The politesse is as functional as it is subtle. Little is known of how it is transmitted. Nor do we understand much better how the "uninstructed" portion of our own culture gets passed on.

We come finally to a consideration of the difficulties and problems one encounters that derive from the educational techniques inherent in "the third way"—teaching by telling out of the context of action. I have tried to consider these in a general sense in "Notes on a Theory of Instruction," and have returned to the specific problem of motivation in "The Will To Learn." Here, I would like to be much more down to earth about the difficulties, to relate them where I can to the specific experience of creating a curriculum, trying it out in teaching, and making an effort to assess it. By an odd historical accident, I am among the small band of scholars who have had

[5] In Bruner, Olver, Greenfield, et al., *Studies in Cognitive Growth.*
[6] For an account of these subtleties, see: Lorna Marshall, "The !Kung Bushmen," in James Gibbs, *The Peoples and Cultures of Africa* (Boston: Houghton Mifflin, 1965); Elizabeth Marshall Thomas, *The Harmless People* (New York: Knopf, 1959), and the film *The Hunters,* made by John Marshall and available through the Peabody Museum of Harvard University.

the sustained experience, as a colleague put it, of going from Widener to Wichita—from the first research in the library to the official launching of the curriculum. I do not make any special claim for the centrality of the topics I wish to consider now, but I think they are typical of what one faces in trying to introduce a new theoretical perspective into the day-to-day operation of schools. For convenience, let me label the problems: the psychology of a subject matter, how to stimulate thought in a school, how to personalize knowledge, and how to evaluate what one is doing.

The psychology of a subject matter. "Subject matters" are an invention of highly literate societies. They can be conceived as ways of thinking about certain phenomena. Mathematics is one way of thinking about order without reference to what is being ordered. The behavioral sciences provide one or perhaps several ways of thinking about man and his society—about regularities, origins, causes, effects. They are probably special (and suspect) because they permit man to look at himself from a perspective that is outside his own skin and beyond his own preferences—at least for a while.

Underlying a discipline's "way of thought," there is a set of connected, varyingly implicit, generative propositions. In physics and mathematics, most of the underlying generative propositions, like the conservation theorems, or the axioms of geometry, or the associative, distributive, and commutative rules of analysis, are by now very explicit indeed. In the behavioral sciences we must be content with greater implicitness. We traffic in inductive propositions: for example, that the different activities of a society are interconnected in such a way that if you know something about the technological response of a society to an environment, you will be able to make some shrewd guesses about its myths or about the things it values. We use the device of significant contrast, as in linguistics, as when we describe the territoriality of a baboon troop in order habitual that it is almost impossible to make quick therapeutic progress in substituting coping for defending where school learning is concerned.

Consider now the nature of therapy. To what extent does therapeutic progress reflect the kind of processes I have been describing? Let me say at the outset that I lay no claim to wide clinical experience with children. Yet I must at least put down the observations we have made and let those with more experience judge their pertinence to the general problems of therapy with children. It has seemed to us in the first place that therapy with our group of children required considerably more than an intrapsychic working through of unconscious material. Working through, yes, particularly if some insight was to be achieved and the constraints of awareness assisted in containing the defensive activity we have described as the preemptive metaphor. But the tutorial was also a crucial factor in helping the child learn to cope. It mattered first in enabling the child to establish a learning situation free of the double bind. Take the eleven-year-old boy who at one of his first sessions said to the tutor that he was afraid to make an error in reading because his teacher yelled at him. The tutor asked whether his teacher yelled very loud, and, upon being assured that she did, volunteered that he could yell louder than the teacher, and urged his patient to make a mistake and see. The boy did, and his tutor in mock voice yelled as loud as he could. The boy jumped. Tutor to patient: "Can she yell louder than that?" Patient: "Yes, lots." Tutor: "Make another error and I'll try to get louder still." The game went on three or four rounds, and the tutor then suggested that the patient try yelling when he, the tutor, made an error. (The tutor was Dr. Michael Maccoby.) After a few sessions, a playful relation had been built up about mistakes in reading, and the beginnings of transference were at hand. Soon the child was able to take satisfaction in the skills in which he was achieving mastery.

The episodes of "sentence craft" and Dick's reaction to them are similarly relevant. Supporting a dependency relationship up to a point—that point being where Dick had to do the actual work of sentence revision himself and judge whether his own performance was correct, the tutor providing the emotional support—had the effect of getting Dick across the line into intrinsic learning. There were comparable episodes in his algebra, where the idea of unknowns to be solved troubled him. Once that was turned into something of a game we played between us, his grasp of the ways of algebra grew on its own. Biology was the next area, and again tutorial therapy ran from initial emotional support to self-propulsion. To be sure, progress was being made at the same time in dealing both with Dick's family situation and with his own intrapsychic conflicts. Yet what was most observable was the manner in which, once tension was reduced, either by means of conventional therapy or the implicit therapy of a supporting tutorial relationship, the child himself would begin to take over and get a sense of reward from such competence as he had managed to establish. If the supporting relationship remained intact, the competence would be extended and the kind of coping necessary to a task would begin in earnest. The tutor as identification figure became increasingly important in all this, for the tutor provided a new model of coping by showing that problems are both soluble and not dangerous —or, when not soluble, at least not the source of either disaster or punishment.

In the end, then, we too were impressed by the sharpness of the difference between coping and defending. When the child could meet the requirements of the tasks set him, the spreading pattern of defense would fade. There was little in common between the two approaches.

What may we conclude about coping and defending?

What seems clearest to me is that there is a deep discontinuity between the two not only in their objectives but also in the nature of the processes involved. Defense, dominated by the need for locating whatever may be disruptive, overshoots its reasonable goal by including in its range anything that can be construed as dangerous. Unconstrained by conscious processes, defense operates by the use of the unlimited and preemptive metaphor—literally a kind of guilt by association that, under extreme stress, finally implicates so much of the patient's world as being potentially dangerous that he is truly crippled. This is the mode of the unconscious, so called. It seems highly unlikely that, on its own, "the unconscious" could be much of a creative source of thinking. Rather more likely, it is only when the metaphoric processes come under conscious control in some degree that they can serve a useful function in coping with problems—what in recent years has been called "regression in the service of the ego."

What seems to be required for a proper growth of respect for the requirements of problem solving is a "defusing" of intellectual activity from the demands of immediate action, affect, and drive. We have suggested that such a defusing depends upon a child's having the conditions necessary for playfulness to develop, upon his having an adequate competence model available, and upon the experience of intrinsic reward from increased competence that can start a career of "learning for its own sake." These produce coping.

There is a form of pedagogical romanticism that urges an arousal of unconscious, creative impulses in the child as an aid to learning. One would do well to be cautious about such doctrine. As Lawrence Kubie and others have remarked, unconscious impulses unconstrained by awareness and by the sense of play can be quite the contrary of creative. It is too often taken for granted that the processes that lead to effective cognitive functioning are mere extensions of unconscious dream work and association. I do not believe this to be the case, and a close reading of Freud certainly indicates that he did not believe so. The "primary process" of infantile thinking was surely not for Freud the basis of later, more world-oriented "secondary process."

In a word, then, coping and defending are not, in my opinion, processes of the same kind that differ merely in degree. They differ in kind. What poses the eternal challenge to the teacher is the knowledge that the metaphoric processes can, when put under the constraints of conscious problem solving, serve the interests of healthy functioning. Without those constraints, they result in the crippling decline that comes from a specialization on defense.

A Retrospect on Making and Judging

IN THE foregoing essays, I have tried to explore the relation between two enterprises, each difficult enough on its own. One is the course of intellectual development, the other pedagogy. In the introductory essay, I sketched how I had become involved in such a joint undertaking. A decade ago, when I first became engaged in this work, it seemed obvious enough to me, as to others, that the two domains must be related, and it was my hope that, betimes, the relation would become clear to me. Indeed, the various essays in this book were attempts to bring some order to the vexed problem of the relation between pedagogy and intellectual development, how the one might assist the other.

What must be plain in the preceding chapters is that the issues to be faced are far broader than those conventionally comprised in what is called "education" or "child rearing." Our proper subject is, of course, how a culture is transmitted —its skills, values, style, technology, and wisdom—and how, in transmission, it produces more effective and zestful human beings. Can we gain some perspective on the matter by examining the evolution of such transmission?

It is, of course, impossible to reconstruct the evolution in techniques of instruction in the shadow zone between early hominids and present man. I have tried to compensate by observing contemporary analogues of earlier forms, knowing full well that the pursuit of analogy can be dangerously misleading. I have spent many hours observing uncut films of the behavior of free-ranging baboons, films shot in East Africa by my colleague Professor Irven DeVore with a very generous footage devoted to infants and juveniles. I have also had access to the unedited film archives of a hunting-gathering people living under roughly analogous ecological conditions, the !Kung Bushman of the Kalahari, recorded by Laurance and Lorna Marshall, brilliantly aided by their son John and daughter Elizabeth. I have also worked directly but informally with the Wolof of Senegal, observing children in the bush and in French-style schools. Even more valuable than my own informal observations in Senegal were the systematic experiments carried out later by my colleague, Patricia Marks Greenfield.[1]

Let me describe very briefly some salient differences in the free learning patterns of immature baboons and among !Kung children. Baboons have a highly developed social life in their troops, with well-organized and stable dominance patterns. They live within a territory, protecting themselves from predators by joint action of the strongly built, adult males. It is striking that the behavior of baboon juveniles is shaped principally by play with their peer group, play that provides opportunity for the spontaneous expression and practice of the component acts that, in maturity, will be orchestrated into the behavior either of the dominant male or of the infant-protective female. All this seems to be accomplished with little participation by any mature animals in the play of the juveniles. We know from the important experiments of Harlow and his colleagues how devastating a disruption in development can be produced in sub-human primates by interfering with their opportunity for peer-group play and social interaction.[2]

Among hunting-gathering humans, on the other hand, there

[1] See Dr. Greenfield's chapters in Bruner, Olver, Greenfield et al., *Studies in Cognitive Growth* (New York: John Wiley & Sons, 1966).
[2] H. Harlow and Margaret Harlow, "Social Deprivation in Monkeys," *Scientific American,* November 1962.

is *constant* interaction between adult and child, adult and adolescent, adolescent and child. !Kung adults and children play and dance together, sit together, participate in minor hunting together, join in song and storytelling together. At very frequent intervals, moreover, children are party to rituals presided over by adults—minor, as in the first haircutting, or major, as when a boy kills his first kudu buck and goes through the proud but painful process of scarification. Children, besides, are constantly playing imitatively with the rituals, implements, tools, and weapons of the adult world. Young juvenile baboons, on the other hand, almost never play with things or imitate directly large and significant sequences of adult behavior.

Note, though, that in tens of thousands of feet of !Kung film, one virtually never sees an instance of "teaching" taking place outside the situation where the behavior to be learned is relevant. Nobody teaches in our prepared sense of the word. There is nothing like school, nothing like lessons. Indeed, among the !Kung there is very little "telling." Most of what we would call instruction is through showing. And there is no practice or drill as such save in the form of play modeled directly on adult models—play hunting, play bossing, play exchanging, play baby tending, play house making. In the end, every man in the culture knows nearly all there is to know about how to get on with life as a man, and every woman as a woman—the skills, the rituals and myths, the obligations and rights.

The change in the instruction of children in more complex societies is twofold. First of all, there is knowledge and skill in the culture far in excess of what any one individual knows. And so, increasingly, there develops an economical technique of instructing the young based heavily on *telling* out of context rather than *showing* in context. In literate societies, the practice becomes institutionalized in the school or the teacher. Both promote this necessarily abstract way of instructing the young.

The result of "teaching the culture" can, at its worst, lead to the ritual, rote nonsense that has led a generation of critics to despair. For, in the detached school, what is imparted often has little to do with life as lived in the society except in so far as the demands of school are of a kind that reflect *indirectly* the demands of life in a technical society. But these indirectly imposed demands may be the most important feature of the detached school. For school is a sharp departure from indigenous practice. It takes learning, as we have noted, out of the context of immediate action just by dint of putting it into a school. This very disengagement makes learning become an act in itself, freed from the immediate ends of action, preparing the learner for the chain of reckoning remote from payoff that is needed for the formulation of complex ideas. At the same time, the school (if successful) frees the child from the pace setting of the round of daily activity. If the school succeeds in avoiding a pace-setting round of its own, it may be one of the great agents for promoting reflectiveness. Moreover, in school, one must "follow the lesson," which means one must learn to follow either the abstraction of written speech—abstract in the sense that it is divorced from the concrete situation to which the speech might originally have been related—or the abstraction of language delivered orally but out of the context of an on-going action. Both of these are highly abstract uses of language.

It is no wonder, then, that many recent studies report large differences between "primitive" children who are in schools and their brothers who are not: differences in perception, abstraction, time perspective, and so on. I need only cite the work of Biesheuvel in South Africa,[3] Gay and Cole in Liberia,[4]

[3] S. Biesheuvel, "Psychological Tests and Their Application to Non-European Peoples," in *The Yearbook of Education* (London: Evans Brothers, 1949), pp. 87–126.

[4] J. Gay and M. Cole, "Outline of General Report on Kpelle Mathematics Project," mimeographed, n.d.

Greenfield in Senegal, Maccoby and Modiano in rural Mexico, Reich among Alaskan Eskimos.[5]

I shall not pause here to consider what is involved in the first two ways of becoming a grown organism—either growing up baboon or growing up in an indigenous society. The latter has had its share of attention in the literature on culture and personality. Even so, there has been little enough effort expended in trying to understand in some decently detailed way how a young man, say, learns not only to hunt but to recognize the necessary blend of technique and ritual—learns the pattern of sharing as well as of hunting. The Bushman, for example, knows extraordinarily exquisite rules about how meat is to be shared after a hunt—what is his own share, what belongs to the owner of the arrow that was "lent" to him as a gift, what belongs to this kinsman and that, and so forth.[6] The politesse is as functional as it is subtle. Little is known of how it is transmitted. Nor do we understand much better how the "uninstructed" portion of our own culture gets passed on.

We come finally to a consideration of the difficulties and problems one encounters that derive from the educational techniques inherent in "the third way"—teaching by telling out of the context of action. I have tried to consider these in a general sense in "Notes on a Theory of Instruction," and have returned to the specific problem of motivation in "The Will To Learn." Here, I would like to be much more down to earth about the difficulties, to relate them where I can to the specific experience of creating a curriculum, trying it out in teaching, and making an effort to assess it. By an odd historical accident, I am among the small band of scholars who have had

[5] In Bruner, Olver, Greenfield, et al., *Studies in Cognitive Growth.*
[6] For an account of these subtleties, see: Lorna Marshall, "The !Kung Bushmen," in James Gibbs, *The Peoples and Cultures of Africa* (Boston: Houghton Mifflin, 1965); Elizabeth Marshall Thomas, *The Harmless People* (New York: Knopf, 1959), and the film *The Hunters,* made by John Marshall and available through the Peabody Museum of Harvard University.

the sustained experience, as a colleague put it, of going from Widener to Wichita—from the first research in the library to the official launching of the curriculum. I do not make any special claim for the centrality of the topics I wish to consider now, but I think they are typical of what one faces in trying to introduce a new theoretical perspective into the day-to-day operation of schools. For convenience, let me label the problems: the psychology of a subject matter, how to stimulate thought in a school, how to personalize knowledge, and how to evaluate what one is doing.

The psychology of a subject matter. "Subject matters" are an invention of highly literate societies. They can be conceived as ways of thinking about certain phenomena. Mathematics is one way of thinking about order without reference to what is being ordered. The behavioral sciences provide one or perhaps several ways of thinking about man and his society—about regularities, origins, causes, effects. They are probably special (and suspect) because they permit man to look at himself from a perspective that is outside his own skin and beyond his own preferences—at least for a while.

Underlying a discipline's "way of thought," there is a set of connected, varyingly implicit, generative propositions. In physics and mathematics, most of the underlying generative propositions, like the conservation theorems, or the axioms of geometry, or the associative, distributive, and commutative rules of analysis, are by now very explicit indeed. In the behavioral sciences we must be content with greater implicitness. We traffic in inductive propositions: for example, that the different activities of a society are interconnected in such a way that if you know something about the technological response of a society to an environment, you will be able to make some shrewd guesses about its myths or about the things it values. We use the device of significant contrast, as in linguistics, as when we describe the territoriality of a baboon troop in order to help us recognize the system of reciprocal exchange of a human group, the former somehow provoking awareness of the latter.

There is nothing more central to a discipline than its way of thinking. There is nothing more important in its teaching than to provide the child the earliest opportunity to learn that way of thinking—the forms of connection, the attitudes, hopes, jokes, and frustrations that go with it. In a word, the best introduction to a subject is the subject itself. At the very first breath, the young learner should, we think, be given the chance to solve problems, to conjecture, to quarrel, as these are done at the heart of the discipline. But, you will ask, how can this be arranged?

Here again the problem of conversion. There exist ways of thinking characteristic of different stages of development. In earlier essays, much has been said about the enactive, iconic, and symbolic modes of representing ideas—particularly in "Notes on a Theory of Instruction." In creating a course, the problem of finding embodiments of ideas in these modes is, of course, central to the idea of the "psychology of a subject matter." So, plainly, the "psychology of a subject matter" is very close to the subject matter itself, and when one speaks of the "psychology of mathematics," it is an enterprise as close to mathematics as it is to psychology. For it matters not whether a mathematical idea finds expression in one notation or another —it must still be a "true" notation. One notational system may be more powerful than another, as already noted, or more apposite to the skills of a child of a certain age. But, in each instance, the mathematics must be decent mathematics. What the psychologist can do is to help invent ways of expressing the ideas so as better to fit the needs of a learner. One can, for example, teach many of the same mathematical ideas in a spatialized iconic form (as with Venn diagrams) or in propositional form (as with the use of truth tables). That is to say, one can "visualize" the statement "if *a* then *b*" as a circle, *a*, within a larger circle, *b*. Or one can "symbolize" it by the statement:

> (*a* and *b*) is true
> (*a* and not-*b*) is false
> (not-*a* and *b*) is true
> (not-*a* and not-*b*) is true

Or, to put it in ordinary language, let (a ⊃ b) stand for:

> If it rains the sidewalks will be wet.

Now the four forms of the truth table are as follows:

> Rain and wet sidewalks are possible.
> Rain and not-wet sidewalks are impossible.
> No rain and wet sidewalks are possible.
> No rain and not-wet sidewalks are possible.

Each mode has its virtues, viewed from a mathematical point of view. In the psychology of mathematics, the task is to delineate the virtues of the two modes (and their interaction) from the point of view of the learner or the user of mathematics.

In our course of study, "Man," there are versions of the subject appropriate to a particular age or a particular stage of learning that can at a later age be given a more powerful or more symbolic rendering. We have tried to choose topics with this in mind: the analysis of kinship that begins with children using sticks and blocks and colors and whatnot to represent their own families, goes on to the conventional general kinship diagrams by a meandering path, and then on to more formal and powerful componential analysis. So too with myth. We begin with the excitement of a powerful myth (like the Netsilik Nuliajik myth), then have the children construct some myths of their own, then examine what a set of Netsilik myths have in common, which takes us finally to Lévi-Strauss's analysis of contrastive features in myth construction.[7] Our difficulty with the "psychology of the behavioral sciences" was that no work existed to guide us. The commonsense "how to solve it" books in mathematics or the more sophisticated works on mathematical heuristics have no counterpart. In effect, we had to build the field as we went, and often in an *ad hoc* way that would probably not bear the close scrutiny of our more demanding colleagues. We consoled ourselves with the thought that shipwrecked sailors do not worry about the opinions of naval architects when they construct their escape rafts.

Thought in the classroom. Consider now our second problem: how to stimulate thought in the setting of a school. We know from experimental studies like those of Bloom and Broder[8] and of Goodnow and Pettigrew[9] that there is a striking difference in the acts of a person who thinks that the task before him represents a problem to be solved and not that it is controlled by random forces. School is a peculiar subculture where such matters are concerned. By school age, children have come to expect quite arbitrary and, from their point of view, meaningless demands to be made upon them by adults— the result, most likely, of the fact that adults often fail to recognize the task of conversion necessary to make their questions have some intrinsic significance for the child. Children, of course, will try to solve problems if they recognize them as such. But they are not often either predisposed to or skillful in problem *finding*, in recognizing the hidden conjectural feature

[7] Claude Lévi-Strauss, *Structural Anthropology,* trans. by Claire Jacobson and Brooke Grundfest Schoepf (New York: Basic Books, 1963).

[8] B. S. Bloom and L. J. Broder, *Problem-Solving Processes of College Students* (Chicago: University of Chicago Press, 1950).

[9] J. J. Goodnow and T. F. Pettigrew, "Effect of Prior Patterns of Experience on Strategies and Learning Sets," *Journal of Experimental Psychology,* 49:381–389 (1955).

in tasks set them. But we know now that children in school can quite quickly be led to such problem finding by encouragement and instruction.

The need for this instruction and encouragement and its relatively swift success relates, I suspect, to what psychoanalysts refer to as the guilt-ridden oversuppression of primary process and its public replacement by secondary process. Children, like adults, need reassurance that it is all right to entertain and express highly subjective ideas, to treat a task as a problem where you *invent* an answer rather than *finding* one out there in the book or on the blackboard. With children in elementary school, there is often a need to devise emotionally vivid special games, story-making episodes, or construction projects to re-establish in the child's mind his right not only to have his own private ideas but to express them in the public setting of a classroom.

But there is another, perhaps more serious difficulty: the interference of extrinsic with intrinsic problem solving. Young children in school expend extraordinary time and effort figuring out what it is that the teacher wants—and usually coming to the conclusion that she or he wants tidiness or remembering or doing things at a certain time in a certain way. This I have referred to in earlier chapters as extrinsic problem solving. There is a great deal of it in school.

There are several quite straightforward ways of stimulating problem solving. One is to train teachers to want it, and that will come in time. But teachers can be encouraged to like it, interestingly enough, by providing them and their children with materials and lessons that *permit* legitimate problem solving and permit the teacher to recognize it. For exercises with such materials create an atmosphere by treating things as instances of what *might* have occurred rather than simply as what did occur. Let me illustrate by a concrete instance. A fifth grade class was working on the organization of a baboon troop—on this particular day, specifically on how they might protect against predators. They saw a brief sequence of film in which six or seven adult males go forward to intimidate and hold off three cheetahs. The teacher asked what the baboons had done to keep the cheetahs off, and there ensued a lively discussion of how the dominant adult males, by showing their formidable mouthful of teeth and making threatening gestures, had turned the trick. A boy raised a tentative hand and asked whether cheetahs always attacked together. Yes, though a single cheetah sometimes followed behind a moving troop and picked off an older, weakened straggler or an unwary, straying juvenile. "Well, what if there were four cheetahs and two of them attacked from behind and two from in front. What would the baboons do then?" The question could have been answered empirically and the inquiry ended. Cheetahs *don't* attack that way, and so we don't know what baboons *might* do. Fortunately, it was not. For the question opens up the deep issues of what might be and why it isn't. Is there a necessary relation between predators and prey that share a common ecological niche? Must their encounters have a "sporting chance" outcome? It is such conjecture, in this case quite unanswerable, that produces rational, self-consciously problem-finding behavior so crucial to the growth of intellectual power. Given the materials, given some background and encouragement, teachers like it as much as the students.

To isolate the major difficulty, then, I would say that while a body of knowledge is given life and direction by the conjectures and dilemmas that brought it into being and sustained its growth, pupils who are being taught often do not have a corresponding sense of conjecture and dilemma. The task of the curriculum maker and teacher is to provide exercises and occasions for its nurturing. If one only thinks of materials and content, one can all too easily overlook the problem. I believe that it is precisely because instruction takes the form of telling-

out-of-the-context-of-action that the difficulty emerges. It is a
pitfall of instruction by the "third way." The answer is the
design of exercises in conjecture, in ways of inquiry, in problem
finding. It is something that the good teacher does naturally at
least some of the time. With help from the curriculum maker's
exercises and conjectures, it is something that ordinary teachers
will do much more of the time.

The personalization of knowledge. Let me turn now to a
third problem, one that is particularly important in social
studies: the personalization of knowledge, getting to the child's
feeling, fantasies, and values with one's lessons. A generation
ago, the progressive movement urged that knowledge be related to child's own experience and brought out of the realm of
empty abstractions. A good idea was translated into banalities
about the home, then the friendly postman and trashman, then
the community, and so on. It is a poor way to compete with
the child's own dramas and mysteries. A decade ago, my colleague Clyde Kluckhohn wrote a prize-winning popular book
on anthropology with the entrancing title *Mirror for Man.* In
some deep way, there is extraordinary power in "that mirror
which other civilizations still hold up to us to recognize and
study . . . [the] image of ourselves."[10] The psychological bases
of the power are not obvious. Is it as in discrimination learning, where increasing the degree of contrast helps in the
learning of a discrimination, or as in studies of concept
attainment, where a negative instance demonstrably defines
the domain of a conceptual rule? Or is it some primitive identification? All these miss one thing that seems to come up fre-
quently in our interviews with the children. It is the experience
of discovering kinship and likeness in what at first seemed
bizarre, exotic, and even a little repellent.

Consider two examples, both involving film of the Netsilik.
In the films, a single nuclear family, Zachary, Marta, and their

[10] Claude Lévi-Strauss, Smithsonian Centennial Lecture, Washington,
D.C., September 1965.

four-year-old Alexei, is followed through the year—spring sealing, summer fishing at the stone weir, fall caribou hunting, early winter fishing through the ice, winter at the big ceremonial igloo. Children report that at first the three members of the family look weird and uncouth. In time, they look normal, and eventually, as when Marta finds sticks around which to warp her braids, the girls speak of how pretty she is. That much is superficial—or so it seems. But consider a second episode.

It has to do with Alexei, who, with his father's help, devises a snare and catches a gull. There is a scene in which he stones the gull to death. Our children watched, horror-struck. One girl, Kathy, blurted out, "He's not even human, doing that to the seagull." The class was silent. Then another girl, Jennine, said quietly: "He's got to grow up to be a hunter. His mother was smiling when he was doing that." And then an extended discussion about how people have to do things to learn and even do things to learn how to feel appropriately. "What would you do if you had to live there? Would you be as smart about getting along as they are with what they've got?" said one boy going back to the accusation that Alexei was inhuman to stone the bird.

I am sorry it is so difficult to say it clearly. What I am trying to say is that to personalize knowledge one does not simply link it to the familiar. Rather one makes the familiar an instance of a more general case and thereby produces awareness of it. What the children were learning about was not seagulls and Eskimos, but about their own feelings and preconceptions that, up to then, were too implicit to be recognizable to them.

There is, perhaps, another route to personalizing knowledge, and it is one that will repel some scholars. Let me propose a view. Our population becomes increasingly urban, and it is characteristic of urban life that it is marked by a certain protective anonymity. Our great metropolitan areas have not only a problem of urban rot and urban renewal at their centers, but

a problem of increasing blandness and remoteness from life
at their bedroom-suburban peripheries. The close-knit, nearby,
extended family of grandparents and maiden aunts of the
small towns and farms is almost extinct. For the middle class
—which is, thanks to our genius in the distribution of wealth,
increasingly large and dominant—there is a remoteness from
the immediate tragic forces in life, a remoteness that is reinforced by the great cosmetic urge of our mass media of communication, our advertisers, our very affluence. We may be
suffering a loss of moral richness at the periphery of our cities.
At the center, in our slums, the problem is quite different and
in the short run far more serious: it is a problem of loss of hope.
Why should the Negro child in central Harlem take the school
as a vehicle to salvation? To him, school is an abstract and an
alien proposition. What has it to do with him, his life, his
aspirations?

Yet, for all our deep worry over hopelessness in the city and
suburban provincialism outside, neither seems to blunt one particular human capacity that overrides both: the sense of drama,
the mysterious device by which we represent most vividly the
range of the human condition. I took a group of fourteen-year-
olds to see Peter Ustinov's *Billy Budd* on film. The intensity of
the discussion of moral philosophy on the way home convinced
me that we have overlooked one of our most powerful allies in
keeping alive our engagement in history, in the range of human
life, in philosophy. Drama, the novel, history rendered with
epic aids of its patron goddess Clio, are all built on the paradox
of human choice, on the resolution of alternatives. They are in
the best sense studies in the causes and consequences of choice.
It is in their gripping quality, their nearness to life, that we can,
I would urge, best make personal the dilemmas of the culture,
its aspirations, its conflicts, its terrors. I should like to propose
that we examine afresh the acting of drama, the use of theater,
the examination of the mythic and the tragic and the comic in

their most powerful expressions. In some considerable measure we have intellectualized and made bland and good-natured the teaching of the particulars of history, of society, of myth. I would urge that in fashioning the instruction designed to give children a view of the different faces and conditions of man, we consider more seriously the use of this most powerful impulse to represent the human condition in drama and, thereby, the drama of the human condition.

Just as concepts and theory serve to connect the facts of observation and experiment in the conventional disciplines of knowledge, so the great dramatic themes and metaphors provide a basis for organizing one's sense of man, for seeing what is persistent in his history and his condition, for introducing some unity into the scatter of our knowledge as it relates to ourselves.

Evaluation. Let me turn next to a problem first raised in the discussion of education as social invention—the question of evaluation. The comment was made there that a curriculum was often evaluated after those who were constructing it had finished their job and folded their tents. It has been our painfully achieved conclusion that if evaluation is to be of help it must be carried out to provide feedback at a time and in a form that can be useful in the design of materials and exercises.

But it is not obvious what the "right time" is or what form of information is the most helpful. I found myself sufficiently puzzled after a year or two of curriculum work to feel the need for setting down guidelines or a "philosophy" of evaluation. I quote directly from a memorandum that followed a first intensive workshop given over to exploring the problem of evaluating a course of study.

1. *Evaluation is best looked at as a form of educational intelligence for the guidance of curriculum construction and pedagogy.* The earlier in the curricular effort intelligence operations begin, the more likely are they to be of use. Effective

evaluation should provide corrective information, but it should also provide informative hypotheses about how to proceed. Indeed, the sensible plan is to start gathering useful information as a *guide to the planning* of a curriculum. To design a course in American history, one would be aided by knowing the historical conceptions of children of the age to be instructed: what are their conceptions of historical cause and effect, their concepts of historical time, their ideas about revolution, and so on. In no sense can such "scouting" determine the specific materials to be used; but it can pose the instructional problems to be solved.

2. *Evaluation, to be effective, must at some point be combined with an effort to teach so that the child's response to a particular process of teaching can be evaluated.* Evaluation should examine not only the product or content of learning but also the process by which the child gets or fails to get to mastery of materials, for only in that way can the efficacy of pedagogy be examined. Content cannot be divorced from pedagogy. For it is the pedagogy that leads the child to treat content in critical ways that develop and express his skills and values. The "instructional interview," of which more will be said later, was designed precisely to assess how a child makes materials his own and how he puts the materials to use in his thinking.

3. *Evaluation can be of use only when there is a full company on board, a full curriculum-building team consisting of the scholar, the curriculum maker, the teacher, the evaluator, and the students.* Its effectiveness is drastically reduced when it is used for the single purpose, say, of editing a chapter, making a film, devising a text. For a curriculum is a thing in balance that cannot be developed first for content, then for teaching method, then for visual aids, then for some other particular feature. The essence of evaluation is that it permits a general shaping of the materials and methods of instruction in a fashion that meets the needs of the student, the criteria of the scholar

from whose discipline materials have been derived, and the needs of the teacher who seeks to stimulate certain ways of thought in his or her pupils.

4. *Evaluation, in its very nature, is likely to create suspicion and concern in the conventional educational setting where it has a history that is inappropriate to present practice of the kind being discussed here.* Evaluation is often viewed as a test of effectiveness or ineffectiveness—of materials, teaching methods, or whatnot—but this is the least important aspect of it. The most important is to provide intelligence on how to improve these things. Many curriculum makers and teachers also know that the results of conventional evaluation can be strikingly affected by the nature of the tests one uses. There is usually some test that can be devised to show that a given curriculum is "working." It is perhaps for this reason that evaluation has had so little effect upon curriculum making even on the rare occasions when the former has been put to use in behalf of the latter. It is crucial to discover an adequate working relationship between evaluator, curriculum maker, and teacher so that they can benefit from each other's activities. One of the important objectives of any evaluation study should be to discover how this can be done. Our experience suggests that the key may be the day-to-day planning and communication of the curriculum-building team that includes the scholar, teacher, evaluator, and students. We have also learned that it is often much the better part of wisdom to design evaluation as a guide to the *preparation* of a later edition, rather than to use it as a basis for polishing a present version of a curriculum. The closer evaluation is to the end of the process, the more it becomes a "test" of a completed product, with all that implies in defensive vanity all round.

5. *From time to time the evaluator must design instruction as a means of probing and developing general intellectual skills.* These skills are not closely and immediately related to any

particular subject matter, but rather to all. One such skill is the utilization of documents; another is the process of making inferences on the basis of minimal information; still another is the development of a sense of responsibility for the implications of one's conclusions; and so on. In such cases it becomes necessary for the evaluator to work jointly with such substantive specialists as he needs in order to ensure that the skills in question are properly developed. Often such skills are, when undeveloped, the real obstacles to the learning of substantive materials.

6. *A curriculum cannot be evaluated without regard to the teacher who is teaching it and the student who is learning it.* The idea of "teacherproof" or "studentproof" material is not only wrong but mischievous. There are some obvious and some not very obvious reasons for this conclusion. Teachers can make or break materials by their attitude toward them and their pedagogical procedures—often more implicitly than explicitly exercised. No matter how well the material may be "presented" by the curriculum maker, it may be over the head of teacher and student alike, producing in the end a misconception. A curriculum, though it represents a body of knowledge, is itself by definition sequential and cannot be evaluated without regard to its sequential nature; yet, in describing it outside the context of teaching, we almost invariably falsify it by the synoptic summary. Learning and teaching, finally, are processes that depend upon a contingent link between a teaching source and a learner. It is for all these reasons that teacher and student are indispensable members of the evaluation enterprise.

7. *Curriculum evaluation must, to be effective, contribute to a theory of instruction.* If it does not, if it is an operation either for reporting what students or teachers say or do or for providing unspecified tidings of success or failure, then it cannot contribute to the aims of the educational enterprise. Those

aims center upon the problem of assisting the development of human beings so that they can use their potential powers to achieve a good life and make an effective contribution to their society. When one loses sight of that objective, both education and its evaluation become technical and sterile. The task of understanding how human beings, in fact, can be assisted in their learning and development is the central task of a theory of instruction, and techniques of evaluation derive from it in the same way that the practice of medicine derives from the medical sciences.

It is one thing to enunciate a set of guidelines; quite another to implement them. Some ills can be treated swiftly. We could at least change the name of the operation, for "evaluation" does not catch the spirit of what was proposed in the memorandum. Accordingly, those of us who had been working on the evaluation of the course on Man began to refer to the operation as "instructional research." But a year later, two perceptive members of the "Instructional Research Group," as it came to be called, could write: "An evaluative branch of any organization is likely to be suspect. Even the Supreme Court is not always able to keep out of trouble."[11]

The swift and cosmetic treatment of name-changing did not work. Indeed, the source of suspicion lies, I think, in the lack of understanding of the nature of evaluation—by whatever name it is called.

Let me say a word about some of the procedures that have come to be used, sometimes with considerable effectiveness, in making plain our pedagogical progress.

The first and perhaps most useful procedure devised was the instructional interview already mentioned. It is instruction, carried out with an individual pupil or small group, that has as

[11] Margaret Donaldson and Mary Henle, "Instructional Research: A Self-Examination Packet," Educational Services, Inc., Social Studies Program, 1965.

its object not simply to teach but also to provide information about how children are learning particular materials and skills and how we can help them. The instructional interview is a tutorial in which materials and pedagogy are tested by an interviewer-teacher conversant not only with the substantive materials but also with the cognitive processes of children. The same children are interviewed repeatedly over varying numbers of sessions; to them it is a form of instruction. What is particularly valuable about this form of interviewing is that it permits a working colloquy to develop between teacher, scholar, and evaluator—with the evaluator then enabled to go back to the children to find out what the scholar or teacher needs to know for his next step.

Let me give an example from some systematic interviews carried out by a member of the Instructional Research Group.[12] In the process of preparing a unit on the difference between biological adaptation through morphological change and cultural adaptation through technological change, we discovered an important stumbling block. Children very swiftly grasp the idea of adaptation—but not in terms of a species. "My feet get tough from walking barefoot during the summer," one child assured the interviewer-teacher. It would appear easy enough to go from this intuitive, personal knowledge of adaptation to the idea of a species adapting to its biological niche. But in fact it is not. For there must be added to the picture ideas like random variation in the species, natural selection of the fit variations, and the rest of what we, as scholars steeped in Darwinian thinking, too easily take for granted. In the end, the warning from the instructional interviews not only saved trouble, but pointed to the necessity of dealing with adaptation in a biologically more comprehensive fashion.

We have found that one other form of inquiry is needed to aid in the intelligence operation. It is designed specifically to

12 I am indebted to Mrs. Marilyn Clayton for the example.

study the linguistic operations of the children exposed to our materials—all of the factors that might affect the comprehension of written materials and of the discussions evoked by these materials. The most revealing study of these factors was undertaken in connection with a junior high school course on Caesar. It is a four-week E.S.I. unit dealing with the Roman crisis of 49 B.C. during which Caesar decided to cross the Rubicon, march down Italy, and wrest power from Pompey. The materials of the course are a selection from Cicero's letters, the first ten or so chapters from Caesar's *Commentaries on the Civil War,* and very brief "background" selections from Plutarch, Suetonius, Lucan, and Polybius—all in English, of course. In addition, there is a relief map of the Italian peninsula and a collection of slides, taken expressly for the course by Jim Burke of *Life* magazine and the classicist Professor Gerald Else of Michigan, following the path of Caesar's march from Ravenna to Brindisi. The method of teaching is Socratic, involving a close and critical reading of texts, maps, and pictures.

The "tryout" of the course in which a pilot evaluation was undertaken was in the form of a seminar of six pupils in the seventh and eighth grades of Boston public schools. The seminar, taught by Mr. Richard Emmett, Jr., of Browne and Nichols School in Cambridge, went on daily for an hour, five days a week for four weeks. The linguistic observations and experiments were carried out by Professor David McNeill, then of Harvard, now of Michigan.[13] McNeill puts the problem succinctly:

"The basic skill, supporting all others, is reading critically. 'Critical' is not the name for what I mean, but I have been unable to think of a better one. Critical reading is not the same as reading fluently. It is, instead, something like the ability to see

[13] See R. S. Emmett, Jr., "Report on the Caesar Unit," Occasional Paper #1, March 1965, Educational Services, Inc., Cambridge, Massachusetts, and David McNeill, "Some Linguistic Skills for History Students," Occasional Paper #2, March 1965, Educational Services, Inc., Cambridge, Massachusetts.

the connotations of sentences. The critical reader gets beyond the material literally referred to and perceives that the sentence is relevant to a larger domain. My assumption is that the parallel between critical reading and formal reasoning is very close. The literal contents of sentences are premises; the connotations are the conclusions. The problem for the student who would become a critical reader is to treat sentences as premises on which to base conclusions, a problem which is complicated by the fact that propositions in sentences are rarely arranged in syllogistic form. Moreover, there is nothing in the sentence itself which triggers this realization of connotation, so the difficulty of alerting students to connotation is formidable."[14]

McNeill then illustrates by taking a sentence and showing its richness of connotation: "Several Pompeian contingents swelled Caesar's ranks and others increased his cavalry strength." Nothing direct is said about the loyalty of Pompey's troops, nor are there grammatical rules for ferretting out connotations of this sort.

What McNeill did was to present the pupils in the class with direct quotations from materials they were familiar with and then have them answer a series of questions about their connotations. His conclusion need not concern us here—that eleven- and twelve-year-olds cannot, save in quite simple instances, use written sentences as premises from which to draw connotative conclusions. What is of interest is the style and nature of the research. For what we learn is the troubles one encounters in dealing with materials that are "told" rather than "shown," and in this case told in written rather than in spoken form.

There is much to be done not only in elucidating the problems of such instruction, but also in designing measures to counteract deficiencies. Does one stimulate more power of connotative leaping by giving children a chance to practice it in

14 McNeill, "Some Linguistic Skills," p. 11.

gamelike forms? "If the following statement is true, how many of the ones following that could also be true? How many are surely false?"

One final point about the issue of evaluation. It has to do with "measurement" in the classic psychometric sense and the relation of such measurement to theory. The comment has been made before—indeed, even in these pages—that measurement follows understanding. If we have a sense of what is worth measuring, we shall measure better. There exists today a pragmatic sense of how, on a broad scale, to measure the success of a particular curriculum—or even how it is working in a given region or for a particular group of children. The pragmatism will one day be converted into a more systematic way of proceeding, and that day will be hastened if we take seriously the task of building a theory of instruction.

The essays that compose this volume are gropings in that direction. They are marred by the fault of too little data, too little systematic observation, too sparse an arsenal of analytic tools. The coming quarter century is likely to be the first in which schools and schooling will be subjected to careful and systematic scrutiny. A spirit of innovation is in the land and the funds for research are becoming available. But it would be a mistake to close this volume by repeating the banal motto that more research is needed. Of course more is needed. But, more to the point, what is needed is the daring and freshness of hypotheses that do not take for granted as true what has merely become habitual. I can only hope that in pursuing a theory of instruction we shall have the courage to recognize what we do not understand and to permit ourselves a new and innocent look.

Index

Abramyan, L. A., 108
Abstract, ability to, 65–66
Adaptation, 74
African education, 31
African Mathematics Project, 54
Allport, Gordon, 3
Alternatives: capacity for dealing with, 6, 20; exploration of, 43–44, 49–50
Anderson, Samuel, 56n
Assimilation and avoidance, 139–142
Attention, 114–117
Attneave, F., 11

Baboons, 118, 150–151, 158–159
Balance beam, 45, 59, 63
Bales, R. Freed, 121
Balikci, Asen, 101
Barker, Roger, 125
Beerbohm, Max, 110
Biesheuvel, S., 152
Billy Budd (Melville), dramatization of, 162
Bipedalism, 24
Bloom, B. S., 157
Bohr, Neils, 135
Broder, L. J., 157
Brown, Roger, 15, 52, 98
Burke, Jim, 169
Bushmen, Kalahari, 84–85, 90, 150–151, 153

Caesar, E.S.I. unit on, 169
Change, dealing with, 35–38
Child rearing, course section on, 86–87

Clayton, Marilyn, 168n
Cole, M., 152
Competence: drive, 86, 117–124, 127; models, 123–124, 135–136, 144
Conceptualizing, rational quality of, 2
Conservation: analysis of errors, 7–10; experiments, 7–8, 13, 15–16
Contrast, as pedagogical device, 64, 84, 93–94, 98
Creativity, 147
Crutchfield, Richard, 95
Curiosity, 43, 114–117
Curriculum, 35; projects in mathematics, 54; building procedures, 70–72; project in social studies, 73–101; aims of social studies course, 101; needs, 159, 162–163. *See also* Evaluation

Dante, 112
Deutsch, Martin, 35
Developmental theory: changes in, 22; emphases in, 27–28
DeVore, Irven, 101, 150
Dewey, John, 23
Dialogue, art of, 19
Dienes, Z. P., 56, 66
Discovery, 96
Documentaries, analytic, 100
Drama, 162–163
Duckworth, Eleanor, 56n

Educational psychology, status of, 37